SPIRITUAL PORTALS

SERGIO NAZIR CHAVEZ

CHARISMA HOUSE

While the author has made every effort to provide accurate, up-to-date source information at the time of publication, statistics and other data are constantly updated. Neither the publisher nor the author assumes any responsibility for errors or for changes that occur after publication. Further, the publisher and author do not have any control over and do not assume any responsibility for third-party websites or their content.

For more resources like this, visit MyCharismaShop.com and the author's website at sergionazirchavez.com.

Cataloging-in-Publication Data is on file with the Library of Congress.
International Standard Book Number: 978-1-63641-475-1
E-book ISBN: 978-1-63641-476-8

1 2025
Printed in the United States of America

Most Charisma Media products are available at special quantity discounts for bulk purchase for sales promotions, premiums, fund-raising, and educational needs. For details, call us at (407) 333-0600 or visit our website at charismamedia.com.

*To my Lord, Savior, and King, Jesus Christ: You are my everything.
Without You, I am nothing. Your love, grace, and mercy are the
foundation of my life and the reason this book exists. All glory,
honor, and praise belong to You alone.*

*To my greatest earthly blessing, my wife, Franchesca: You are the
embodiment of God's love to me. Your unwavering support and
encouragement have been my anchor. Through you, God has given
me my most precious treasures—our children: Kalea, Nadae, and
Naviyah. Kalea, with your bright spirit; Nadae, with your boundless
curiosity; and Naviyah, with your tender heart—you are my
inspiration, my joy, and the evidence of God's goodness in my life.*

*To Charisma: Thank you for believing in me, for seeing God's grace
in me, and for giving me the opportunity to share this message. Your
trust and support have opened a door I will never take for granted.
This book is for all of you—a reflection of the faith, love, and hope
that have carried me through. May every word honor the One who
deserves it all.*

CONTENTS

Foreword by Ed Citronnelli xi

INTRODUCTION: THE SPIRITUAL REALITY OF PORTALS xv
The Biblical Foundation of Portals xvi
The Purpose of This Book. xvii
A Call to Spiritual Awareness xviii
Activation Prayer xviii

CHAPTER 1: UNDERSTANDING HEAVENLY PORTALS 1
The Nature of Heavenly Portals 2
How to Open Heavenly Portals in Your Life. 6
Activation Prayer 7

CHAPTER 2: UNDERSTANDING DEMONIC PORTALS. 11
The Nature of Demonic Portals. 12
Recognizing Demonic Portals 18
Closing Demonic Portals Through Repentance and
Deliverance 20
Activation Prayer 24

CHAPTER 3: THE BATTLE FOR THE SOUL 27
The Reality of Spiritual Warfare 28
How to Discern and Engage in the Battle for the Soul. 37
Activation Prayer 41

CHAPTER 4: OPENING HEAVENLY PORTALS THROUGH PRAYER. 45
The Power of Prayer in the Spiritual Realm 48
Types of Prayer That Open Heavenly Portals 49
Practical Steps to Cultivate a Prayer Life That Opens
Heavenly Portals 52
Activation Prayer 57

CHAPTER 5: WORSHIP AS A GATEWAY TO THE DIVINE. 61
   Worship That Produces God's Glory. 63
   The Essence of True Worship 66
   The Role of Music and Praise in Worship. 68
   The Power of Sound and Frequency 70
   Creating a Lifestyle of Worship. 72
   Activation Prayer 77

CHAPTER 6: THE WORD OF GOD AS A PORTAL OPENER 81
   The Living Power of God's Word 82
   The Transformative Power of Meditating on the Word. . . . 84
   Speaking and Declaring the Word. 85
   The Word as a Weapon in Spiritual Warfare. 87
   Activation Prayer 90

CHAPTER 7: THE ROLE OF FAITH IN ENGAGING PORTALS 93
   The Foundation of Faith in Engaging Portals 94
   Overcoming Doubt and Unbelief 97
   Practical Ways to Make Faith a Daily Practice 102
   The Reward of Faith 103
   Activation Prayer 104

CHAPTER 8: THE DANGERS OF ENGAGING WITH DEMONIC PORTALS 107
   The Consequences of Opening Demonic Portals. 108
   Recognizing the Signs of a Demonic Portal. 110
   Steps to Close Demonic Portals. 111
   Protecting Yourself and Others from Demonic Portals 113
   Activation Prayer 115

CHAPTER 9: DELIVERANCE AND CLOSING DEMONIC PORTALS 117
   The Biblical Foundation for Deliverance. 118
   Signs That Deliverance May Be Needed 119
   The Process of Deliverance 121
   Leaving the Past Behind 123
   The Role of the Church in Deliverance. 127
   Activation Prayer 128

CHAPTER 10: WALKING IN AUTHORITY OVER PORTALS 131
Understanding Spiritual Authority 132
Exercising Authority to Close Demonic Portals. 134
Encouraging Others to Walk in Authority 137
Activation Prayer 140

CHAPTER 11: CREATING A HEAVENLY PORTAL IN YOUR HOME 143
The Importance of a God-Centered Home 144
Protecting the Spiritual Atmosphere of Your Home 149
Your Home as a Spiritual Legacy. 151
Activation Prayer 152

CHAPTER 12: THE ROLE OF THE CHURCH IN OPENING HEAVENLY PORTALS 155
The Church as a Gateway to Heaven 157
Corporate Worship and the Manifestation of
God's Presence. 157
The Power of Unity in Opening Portals 159
Prayer and Intercession as Portal Openers 160
The Impact of Open Portals on the Church
and the World 161
The Church's Responsibility in
Sustaining Open Portals 163
Activation Prayer 166

CHAPTER 13: GUARDING AGAINST DECEPTION 169
The Reality of Spiritual Deception 170
Developing Discernment 173
The Role of the Holy Spirit in
Guarding Against Deception. 174
Practical Steps to Guard Against Deception 176
The Consequences of Falling into Deception 177
Activation Prayer 180

CHAPTER 14: ENGAGING IN SPIRITUAL WARFARE 183
The Reality of Spiritual Warfare 184
Warfare in the Air (the Arena of Our Thoughts). 185
The Biblical Symbolism of Air. 187

Symbolic Themes of Air 188
Practical Insights into Spiritual Warfare 189
Understanding the Armor of God .189
Strategies for Engaging in Spiritual Warfare 191
Overcoming Fear in Spiritual Warfare. 193
Activation Prayer 195

CHAPTER 15: LIVING IN THE VICTORY OF HEAVENLY PORTALS 197
Understanding Our Victory in Christ 198
Overcoming Challenges to Victory 200
Sharing the Victory with Others .201
Activation Prayer 205

CONCLUSION: DARK NIGHT OF THE SOUL 209
My Own Dark Night of the Soul 210
Lessons from the Dark Night 211
Victory Through the Portal 212

A Personal Note. 215
About the Author. 217

FOREWORD

I⁣T IS WITH great honor and joy that I write this foreword for a work that I believe will profoundly impact the body of Christ. The message of *Spiritual Portals* is one that is both timely and necessary in this critical hour.

The Spirit of the Lord is calling His people to a deeper understanding of His supernatural realm, and this book serves as a road map to access, engage, and sustain that divine connection.

As a spiritual father and mentor to Sergio Nazir Chavez, I have had the privilege of witnessing his remarkable journey of faith and spiritual growth firsthand. Sergio's hunger for God, humility, and passion for advancing the kingdom have been evident throughout the years we've shared together. He is not only a spiritual son but also a fellow laborer in Christ, and it brings me great joy to see him walking boldly in the call God has placed on his life. This book is a testament to that calling—a profound outpouring of divine revelation rooted in intimacy with the Holy Spirit.

Having been in ministry for over twenty years, with extensive experience in the realms of the supernatural and deliverance, I can truly connect with the truths presented in *Spiritual Portals*. Over the years, I have seen the urgency for believers to embrace the supernatural dimensions of God's kingdom. This book provides not only a theological foundation but also practical insights that equip readers to engage with these realities effectively. Sergio has poured his heart into every page, offering a wealth of wisdom, personal testimonies, and biblical principles that will empower you to live victoriously.

As believers, we are called not to live in defeat or uncertainty but in the fullness of the victory that Christ has already won for us. This book does not merely present theoretical knowledge; it is born out of lived experiences, battles fought, and victories won. From understanding spiritual authority to engaging in warfare, from opening heavenly portals to guarding against deception, every chapter is designed to equip you for a victorious walk with Christ.

Reflecting on the powerful principles shared in this book, I am reminded of the words of Jesus in John 14:12: "Very truly I tell you, whoever believes in me will do the works I have been doing, and they will do even greater things than these, because I am going to the Father." This is not a distant promise—it is a reality that we are invited to live out through faith, obedience, and the empowerment of the Holy Spirit.

This book challenges us to move beyond a passive Christianity into an active, vibrant faith that changes atmospheres, shifts destinies, and impacts the world around us. It calls us to walk boldly in our identity as children of God, to engage in spiritual warfare with confidence, and to open portals that bring heaven to earth.

As you read these pages, I encourage you to approach them with an open heart and a hunger for more of God. Allow the Holy Spirit to guide you, to reveal truths that will transform your life, and to ignite a fire within you that cannot be extinguished. This is not just a book—it is an invitation to step into the supernatural dimensions of God's kingdom and to live in the fullness of His victory.

Sergio, my beloved son in the faith, I am deeply honored to contribute to this work. The anointing on your life, the depth of revelation God has entrusted to you, and the passion you carry for His kingdom are undeniable. *Spiritual Portals* is not just a book; it is a divine mandate. I am confident that it will awaken hearts, stir faith, and equip believers to step into their divine destinies with boldness.

Dear reader, I pray that as you journey through this work, you will experience breakthroughs, receive divine revelation, and be empowered to fulfill your God-given purpose. May you encounter the glory of God in new and profound ways, and may your life become a living testimony of His power and love.

With great expectation for what God will do through this message,

—Ed Citronnelli

Founder and Senior Leader

World Healing International Ministries

Ed Citronnelli Ministries

THE SPIRITUAL REALITY OF PORTALS

And [he] said, "Look! I see the heavens opened and the
Son of Man standing at the right hand of God."
—Acts 7:56, mev

I N THE VAST expanse of the spiritual realm, a profound yet often misunderstood reality exists: portals. These spiritual gateways serve as channels between the physical world and the spiritual dimensions, influencing our lives in many ways that we cannot always see. To some, the concept of portals may seem foreign or even mystical. Before you dismiss this idea outright, allow me to "break it down" both biblically and experientially.

Many in the body of Christ have been turned off by the term *portals*, largely because it has been mischaracterized as a New Age concept. Unfortunately, this confusion has led to the labeling of a simple English word as part of a heretical or demonic doctrine. Yet, due to this misunderstanding, many believers have unknowingly opened themselves to unnecessary suffering and torment, missing or dismissing their God-given potential as a result. No wonder Hosea 4:6 (NKJV) declares, "My people are destroyed for lack of knowledge."

The Bible provides numerous references and examples that underscore the existence and significance of portals. Throughout Scripture, we witness instances where God opens heavenly portals that allow Him to come down into the lives of His people in a powerful way. But there are also accounts where demonic portals are opened, and darkness and oppression are the result. For every believer who desires to walk in the fullness of God's plan and guard against the enemy's schemes, understanding these portals and their operation is essential.

This book is a journey into the heart of spiritual warfare, exploring the nature of these portals and the profound impact they have on so many areas of our lives.

Together, we will delve into Scripture, drawing from its rich collection of stories and teachings to uncover the truths about heavenly and demonic portals. My goal is to equip you with the knowledge and spiritual tools needed to open these portals and bring down blessings into your life while closing and guarding against any demonic portals that seek to infiltrate your spiritual journey.

The Biblical Foundation of Portals

Portals are not merely the stuff of fantasy or science fiction. They are a very real part of the daily spiritual landscape. In the Bible, one of the most striking examples of a heavenly portal is found in the story of Jacob's ladder in Genesis 28:10–17. As Jacob lay asleep in the wilderness, he had a dream in which he saw a ladder reaching from earth to heaven, with angels ascending and descending on it. Above the ladder stood the Lord, who spoke to Jacob, reaffirming His covenant with him. More than just a dream, this vision was actually a glimpse into the spiritual reality of a heavenly portal—an open connection between heaven and earth through which God's blessings and divine encounters could flow.

Similarly, Jesus Christ describes Himself as the ultimate portal in John 10, declaring, "I am the gate; whoever enters through me will be saved" (v. 9). Jesus is the gateway to eternal life, the door through which we must enter to access the presence of God and the blessings of the kingdom. Through His sacrifice on the cross, He opened the greatest of all heavenly portals, granting us direct access to the Father.

On the other hand, the Bible also warns of the existence of

demonic portals—gateways through which evil can enter and exert influence. One example is the story of Saul and the medium at Endor in 1 Samuel 28. In a moment of desperation, King Saul sought out a medium to summon the spirit of the prophet Samuel, thereby opening a demonic portal that ultimately led to his downfall. This account serves as a sobering reminder of the dangers of engaging with the occult and other practices that open doors to the demonic realm.

The Purpose of This Book

Spiritual Portals is not just a theological study. It is a practical guide for navigating the spiritual realities that hold great influence over your daily life. As we explore the concept of portals, we will provide you with biblical insights and practical strategies to do as follows:

- Recognize and discern the presence of heavenly and demonic portals in your life.

- Engage in spiritual practices that open portals to blessings in your life, including spending time with the Lord in worship and the study of His Word.

- Protect yourself and your loved ones from the influence of demonic portals.

- Walk in the authority given to you by Christ to close demonic portals and establish heavenly ones.

- Harness the creative power of your thoughts and words to close demonic portals that are destroying you and open those portals that will bring you abundant life in Jesus Christ!

Throughout this book I will share testimonies and real-life examples of individuals who have experienced the impact of these portals, both for good and for evil. Some of the people you read about met the destructive consequences of engaging with demonic portals, but there are other stories of miraculous encounters with God through heavenly portals that will encourage you to seek them in your life, along with the blessings that they bring.

A Call to Spiritual Awareness

In an age when the line between the spiritual and the physical is often blurred or ignored, it is vital for believers to be spiritually aware and vigilant. The battle between good and evil is real, and it is fought not just in the physical realm but in the spiritual realm as well. Ephesians 6:12 reminds us, "Our struggle is not against flesh and blood, but against the rulers, against the authorities, against the powers of this dark world and against the spiritual forces of evil in the heavenly realms."

As you embark on this journey through the pages of *Spiritual Portals*, I encourage you to approach it with an open heart and a willingness to learn. The truths you will discover in this book have the potential to transform your spiritual life, equipping you to live with greater spiritual authority and sensitivity.

May this book be a portal of its own—one that opens your eyes to the spiritual realities around you and draws you closer to the heart of God. May you be empowered to shut down any work of the enemy as he seeks to steal, kill, and destroy, and instead receive from God through the portals of blessing and light He opens in your life.

Let us begin this journey together, with the Word of God as our guide and the Holy Spirit as our teacher.

Activation Prayer

Father, I come before You in the name of Jesus Christ with a heart full of gratitude and expectation. I ask that Your Holy Spirit help my mind to understand the teachings You desire to reveal to me through this book. Thank You for Your Word, which is a lamp to my feet and a light to my path. Draw me deeper in my faith. Bring me closer to the heart of Jesus, and awaken a greater sense of Your presence and power in my life.

Lord, I surrender myself completely to You in this moment. Prepare my heart to step into a deeper and greater level of intimacy with You. As I embark on this journey through the truths revealed in Spiritual Portals, I choose to receive fully all that You have in store for me. Father, I boldly declare that I dismantle every plan of the enemy that is not in Your plan for my life. I welcome Your presence to transform every area of my life.

May the living Jesus Christ be glorified in me and through me, not just as I read this book, but as I live out the truths You reveal. Take me beyond the ordinary into the extraordinary dimensions of Your kingdom. Let this be a journey of breakthrough! In Your presence, I know I will find the strength to fulfill all that You have called me to do. Thank You for inviting me into this exciting adventure with You. In Jesus' mighty name, amen.

CHAPTER 1

UNDERSTANDING HEAVENLY PORTALS

THE CONCEPT OF heavenly portals is woven throughout the tapestry of Scripture, revealing the profound ways God interacts with humanity. These portals serve as spiritual gateways, connecting the realm of heaven with the earth, allowing God's power and presence to flow into the lives of believers. I don't know about you, but I want to be a part of anything that increases God's ability to work in my life! It turns out that understanding these portals is essential for anyone who desires to deepen their relationship with God and experience His presence in a tangible way.

Before delving into the nature and significance of heavenly portals, let me share a personal encounter that illuminated this profound concept in my life. It was a summer day during a season marked by intense seeking, fasting, and praying. The Holy Spirit had impressed upon me the need to set aside three days to go to a prayer mountain. He was preparing me for a new work, although I had no idea what was about to unfold.

The journey to the specific location the Holy Spirit directed me to was long and arduous. I traveled for hours, finally arriving at the base of a particular mountain. Exhausted but determined, I began the climb to the exact spot the Holy Spirit had designated. My body was in a fasted state, and I was physically weak. Yet, as I ascended, I felt a growing anticipation in my spirit.

When I reached the destination, I began to worship and pray with all the strength I could muster. As the hours passed, I felt my physical body growing weaker, but my spirit became more attuned to the divine presence surrounding the mountain. Then, for one of the few times in my life, I heard the audible voice of God. It was unlike anything I had ever experienced—a sound both thunderous and deeply intimate.

He said to me, "You are My mouthpiece. You are My prophet."

In that moment, my body trembled, and I fell to my knees in fear, awe, and reverence. Tears streamed down my face as the weight of His words settled in my heart. The Holy Spirit began to bring clarity, connecting all the dots from the season I was in and the calling I was stepping into. It was a divine commissioning into a new office and ministry—a transformation that would change every aspect of my life.

Then came the pivotal question: "My son, do you say yes?"

Weeping, I responded, "My answer is yes."

He revealed to me that this calling would cost me everything. With trembling hands and a resolute heart, I answered again, "I am willing, and my answer is yes."

This encounter was a profound illustration of a heavenly portal being opened. It was a moment of divine connection when heaven invaded earth, bringing clarity, commissioning, and transformation. With that foundation, let us explore the nature and significance of heavenly portals.

The Nature of Heavenly Portals

The heavenly portals I've learned about are *not* physical doors or gates that we can see with the natural eye. They are spiritual openings that we can activate ourselves, and when we do, they allow all kinds of spiritual blessings to pass down from heaven and into our lives—blessings like a greater sense of God's presence, along with healing for our bodies and souls, power to overcome sin, and so much more. How do we activate these portals, allowing God to reach into our lives in a greater way? The pathway for heaven to invade earth opens when we seek His presence more, especially through prayer and meditation on His Word. The idea of portals is a scriptural one. In fact, the Bible provides numerous examples of such portals, demonstrating their significance in the lives of God's people.

One of the most well-known examples of a heavenly portal is found in the story of Jacob's dream at Bethel. As Jacob journeyed to Haran, he stopped to rest for the night, using a stone for a pillow. As he slept, he had a vision of a ladder reaching from earth to heaven. This ladder had many angels ascending and descending on it, moving up and down from heaven to earth and back. At the top of the ladder stood the Lord, who spoke to Jacob, reaffirming His covenant with him and promising to bless him and his descendants. When Jacob awoke, he declared, "Surely the LORD is in this place, and I was not aware of it....How awesome is this place! This is none other than the house of God; this is the gate of heaven" (Gen. 28:16–17).

This passage illustrates the nature of heavenly portals as places of divine encounter. Jacob's dream was not just a symbolic vision. It was an *actual glimpse* into the spiritual reality of a portal that connects heaven and earth. Through this portal Jacob received a revelation of God's presence and His plans for the future. And this portal wasn't just a onetime event. Many of these portals are associated with specific locations, but they can also be opened through the spiritual practices of believers, allowing them to experience God's presence in their daily lives. That means *we* can experience the kind of portal Jacob saw in our own lives!

Heavenly portals are not confined to specific locations or times; they can be opened anywhere and at any time when the conditions are right. When we live our lives close to the Lord, coming to Him in prayer with everything, surrendering our will to His in an attitude of worship, it brings an atmosphere of heaven to the earth. *That* is when He will move in our lives. *That* is when the heavenly portals will open and His blessings will rain down. When believers are fully engaged in their relationship with God, they create an atmosphere conducive to the opening of heavenly portals that will usher the presence of the Lord into their lives.

While there are many examples of heavenly portals in the Bible, none is more significant than Jesus Christ Himself. In the Gospel of John, Jesus made a profound statement about His role as the gateway to the Father: "I am the gate; whoever enters through me will be saved. They will come in and go out, and find pasture" (John 10:9). Here, Jesus identifies Himself as the ultimate portal through which believers can access the presence of God and receive eternal life.

Jesus' declaration highlights the exclusive nature of this heavenly portal—He is the only way to the Father. In John 14:6, He further emphasized this truth, saying, "I am the way and the truth and the life. No one comes to the Father except through me." Through His sacrificial death and resurrection, Jesus opened the greatest of all heavenly portals, providing a direct connection between God and humanity. Those who enter through this portal receive forgiveness, salvation, and the promise of eternal life. (To learn more about how to make Jesus Lord of your life, see my personal note at the end of this book.)

The significance of Jesus as the ultimate portal is further underscored in the Book of Hebrews, where He is described as the Mediator of a new covenant, opening the way for believers to boldly approach the throne of grace: "Therefore, brothers and sisters,...we have confidence to enter the Most Holy Place by the blood of Jesus, by a new and living way opened for us through the curtain, that is, his body" (10:19–20). This passage emphasizes that through Jesus, we have access to the very presence of God—a privilege that was once reserved only for the high priest under the old covenant.

Angels also play a significant role in the operation of heavenly portals, often acting as messengers and agents of God's will. Remember Jacob's dream? Angels were ascending and descending the ladder, but what were they doing? They were moving back and forth between heaven and earth to carry out the plans God sent them to fulfill. Those divine missions are typically the result of the prayers of His people! The Book of Daniel provides another example of angelic activity in relation to heavenly portals.

In Daniel 10, the prophet Daniel had been fasting and praying for three weeks, seeking understanding and revelation from God. On the twenty-first day, he had a vision of an angelic being sent to deliver a message to him. The angel explained that he had been delayed for twenty-one days by the "prince of the Persian kingdom" (v. 13), a demonic entity, until the archangel Michael came to assist him. The angel's words reveal the reality of spiritual warfare at heavenly portals: "Do not be afraid, Daniel. Since the first day that you set your mind to gain understanding and to humble yourself before your God, your words were heard, and I have come in response to them" (v. 12).

This passage illustrates that heavenly portals are not only avenues for divine blessing and revelation but also battlegrounds where spiritual warfare occurs. Angels are dispatched through these portals to bring down God's answers to our prayers, as well as engage in spiritual warfare on our behalf. Understanding the role of angels in relation to heavenly portals can help us pray more effectively and be aware of the spiritual dynamics at play in our lives.

I remember a profound encounter with angelic assistance while preparing to lead a prophetic school. As I prayed and sought God for clarity and direction, I felt an unusual heaviness and discouragement. It seemed as though a spiritual blockage was preventing me from receiving the insight I needed. Despite this, I pressed into prayer, pleading with the Lord for guidance and breakthrough.

One afternoon, while in my bedroom, I felt a wave of drowsiness and drifted into a state between sleep and wakefulness. In this stillness, I sensed a presence surrounding me. At first, I thought it might be one of my daughters, but then I remembered I was alone at home. As I lay there, I felt a physical breeze moving around me, like a fresh wind sweeping through the room.

Startled, I awoke and asked the Lord what had happened. He ministered to my heart, saying, "I sent My messengers with a fresh wind for your assignment." I realized that the presence I felt was angelic—sent to strengthen and prepare me for the prophetic mission I was to fulfill. Immediately after this encounter, clarity flooded my mind. I received divine instruction, words of knowledge, and prophetic insight for the event. My strength was renewed, and I went forth with confidence, knowing I had been equipped by heaven for the task ahead.

This personal experience illustrates the vital role of angels in heavenly portals. They bring divine assistance and strength, especially when believers are weary or in need of direction. Understanding their ministry can encourage us to trust God's provision and to remain steadfast in prayer and faith.

How to Open Heavenly Portals in Your Life

Heavenly portals can be opened in the life of a believer through various spiritual disciplines. Prayer, worship, and the proclamation of God's Word are powerful ways to create an atmosphere that invites the presence of God and opens portals to the divine. The Bible teaches that God inhabits the praises of His people (Ps. 22:3, kjv), and where His presence is welcomed, heavenly portals are opened.

One practical example of this truth is found in the story of Paul and Silas in Acts 16. After being imprisoned for preaching the gospel, Paul and Silas prayed and sang hymns to God. As they worshipped, a powerful earthquake shook the prison's foundations, opening all the doors and loosening everyone's chains (vv. 25–26). This miraculous event was more than just a physical occurrence. A heavenly portal had been opened through their worship, allowing God's power to manifest in the natural realm.

To experience this kind of supernatural power in your life, it is essential to cultivate a lifestyle of prayer and worship. Regularly spending time in God's presence, meditating on His Word, and declaring His promises will create an environment where heavenly portals can be activated. Additionally, living a life of holiness and obedience to God's commands will ensure that the portals you open lead to His blessings and not to spiritual opposition.

Heavenly portals are spiritual gateways that connect the physical realm with the spiritual realm. They aren't just symbolic. They represent God's real and tangible interactions with His people—and that includes you! From the examples of Jacob's dream at Bethel to the ultimate portal found in Jesus Christ, these gateways allow divine power, blessings, and revelation to flow into our lives.

Understanding these portals and how to access them is essential for any believer who desires to experience the fullness of God's presence and power. By engaging in the spiritual practices we discuss throughout this book, such as prayer, worship, and the proclamation of God's Word, we can create environments where heavenly portals are activated, bringing heaven to earth in powerful ways. As we continue to seek God's presence, let us remain open to the divine encounters that await us through these heavenly portals.

Activation Prayer

Heavenly Father, I come before You with a heart full of gratitude for the revelation of Your presence and the divine connection You have made available to me through heavenly portals. Thank You for the examples in Your Word that show me how You interact with humanity and for the ultimate portal, Jesus Christ, through whom I have access to Your throne of grace.

Lord, I ask that You open my spiritual eyes to recognize these portals in my life. Teach me to cultivate a lifestyle of constantly seeking Your face so that Your presence can flow freely into every area of my being. I desire to encounter

You deeply and tangibly, just as Jacob did at Bethel and as others have experienced throughout Scripture.

Strengthen me with Your Spirit, Lord, to press into Your presence even when the journey feels long or the battles seem intense. Just as You sent angels to strengthen and guide in times past, I ask for Your divine messengers to come alongside me, helping me complete the tasks You have called me to fulfill.

Help me walk in the fullness of my identity in Christ, knowing that He is the way, the truth, and the life. May His example guide me as I seek to align my life with Your will and bring Your kingdom to earth through my faith and obedience.

I surrender to You, Lord, and I ask for heavenly portals of blessing to open in every area of my life. Let Your glory shine through me so that others may experience Your power and love. In Jesus' mighty name, I pray. Amen.

DID YOU KNOW?

Brain-imaging studies reveal that moments of awe, wonder, and amazement—like those felt during worship or divine encounters—activate the prefrontal cortex and the limbic system, which are linked to spiritual experiences and emotional connection. This activity mirrors the transformative effect of accessing heavenly portals, where God's glory inspires awe and intimacy!

PORTALS IN POP CULTURE:
The Matrix (1999 film)

Neo's awakening to the "real world" parallels the believer's recognition of spiritual warfare and the unseen battle between good and evil. It's a modern parable about choosing truth and breaking free from deception. In the end, we must choose light over darkness, truth over illusion, and we must open the gates that lead us to deeper dwelling in Christ.

CHAPTER 2

UNDERSTANDING DEMONIC PORTALS

AT THIS POINT, I have established a solid biblical foundation for heavenly portals. I believe you're ready to go deeper!

While heavenly portals allow the flow of God's blessings, guidance, and presence into our lives, there are also demonic portals—dark spiritual gateways that open avenues for evil forces either to oppress us or to harm us outright. We need to understand these portals so we can first recognize them when they are opened—and also so we can resist the enemy by closing them, ensuring that our lives remain under the protective covering of God's grace and truth!

Before diving into the nature of demonic portals, let me share a personal story that revealed the reality of these spiritual gateways in a profound way.

The Lord called me into a time of shutting in for prayer and fasting when my church had just purchased a new facility. He instructed me to separate myself in the sanctuary for five days. "You will not leave the space," He said. "You will sleep in the sanctuary because I will meet you there. Await what I will show you, and obey what I tell you to do."

I obeyed, dedicating myself to prayer and fasting. On the first and second days, I pressed into prayer, seeking the Lord's presence and direction. On the third day, around 3:30 a.m., I had a startling encounter. In a semi-sleep state after hours of intercession, I heard what sounded like a car screeching and crashing—not outside the building but inside, near where I was praying.

The sound jolted me awake, and my body experienced what

many know as sleep paralysis. I immediately recognized that spiritual warfare had begun. The powers ruling over our neighborhood and city—oppressing the community with crime, poverty, addiction, and immorality—had manifested from the spirit realm into my current physical reality.

Although physically paralyzed, I began to call on the name of the Lord in my mind and spirit. I interceded, calling on the angels assigned to our ministry and the power of the Holy Spirit. The Holy Spirit illuminated the specific principalities at work, revealing the strongholds of oppression that had plagued our city, such as Mammon (poverty, oppression, and greed), Belial (rebellion), Molech (violence and death), and Asherah (lust, idolatry).

For hours, I engaged in spiritual warfare. Although my body grew weak, I pressed on, calling on the Lord with fervency. With each prayer, I could feel a tangible lifting. What began as a heavy, oppressive darkness hovering over the building gradually gave way to light and clarity.

At one point, I looked up at the ceiling. Although it was physically intact, I saw in a vision that the spiritual ceiling was opening, and a radiant light shone down from heaven into the sanctuary. At that moment, I knew the answers had come. God's presence filled the room, and the oppressive grip of darkness over the building and our ministry was broken.

This encounter was a vivid demonstration of the reality of demonic portals and the power of prayer and intercession to bring the presence of the Lord, which holds the power to save us and set us free! Now let us explore the nature of demonic portals and how they operate.

The Nature of Demonic Portals

Demonic portals are spiritual gateways that grant access to demonic forces in the lives of individuals, communities, and even nations. These portals can be opened through various means, but sin is almost always the root cause. Sins that are tied to the realm of darkness and the occult seem to have a strong ability to bring that darkness into the lives of those who have "invited" it in through those sins. Unlike heavenly portals, which are opened through faith, prayer, and obedience to God, demonic portals are typically opened through rebellion against God's commandments, involvement in witchcraft or the occult, and persistent sin without repentance.

One of the clearest biblical examples of a demonic portal being opened is found in the story of King Saul and the medium of Endor in 1 Samuel 28. After God refused to answer Saul through traditional means, he sought out a medium to summon the spirit of the prophet Samuel. This act of consulting the dead, known as necromancy, is strictly forbidden in Scripture (Deut. 18:10–12). By engaging in this occult practice, Saul opened a demonic portal, inviting spiritual darkness into his life. The result was disastrous, as Saul's disobedience led to his downfall and ultimately his death.

The story of Saul illustrates the danger of opening demonic portals through sinful actions and disobedience to God. These portals create avenues for demonic forces to gain a foothold in a person's life, and the results are everything the devil loves to propagate in our lives: suppression, oppression, possession, confusion, and destruction. As believers, it is essential to recognize the signs of demonic portals and take steps to close them through repentance and spiritual warfare.

As I have said before, demonic portals are not merely abstract concepts. They operate according to specific spiritual laws that govern the interactions taking place between the natural and spiritual realms. When a person engages in activities contrary to God's commands—especially intentional sin or occult practices—spiritual doors are opened, allowing demonic forces to enter. These forces then seek to establish strongholds in the person's life, manipulating their thoughts, emotions, and actions to align with the kingdom of darkness.

Below are examples of activities that can open demonic portals. These actions are direct violations of God's Word and invite demonic entities to gain influence. Similarly, environments saturated with negative influences—such as certain forms of entertainment that glorify violence or promote immorality or the occult—can also serve as gateways for demonic forces. The Bible warns against allowing such influences into our lives, as seen in Ephesians 4:27, where Paul admonished believers, "Do not give the devil a foothold."

Divination and fortune-telling

Practices aimed at gaining hidden knowledge about the future or unseen realms, such as these:

- Tarot cards
- Crystal ball readings
- Palm reading
- Pendulum dowsing

Biblical warning:

> Let no one be found among you...who practices divination or...interprets omens.
> —DEUTERONOMY 18:10

These practices rely on sources of knowledge apart from God and lead to spiritual deception.

Spirit communication and necromancy

Attempts to contact the dead or spirits for guidance, including these:

- Séances
- Ouija boards
- Mediums and psychics

- Automatic writing (channeling spirits to write messages)

Biblical warning:

> Do not turn to mediums or seek out spiritists, for you will be defiled by them.
> —LEVITICUS 19:31

These practices often invoke demonic forces masquerading as spirits of the dead.

Witchcraft and sorcery

Practices that seek to manipulate reality through rituals, spells, or invoking spiritual powers, which could include the following:

- Casting spells or hexes

- Wicca rituals

- Love spells or binding spells

- Using talismans, amulets, or charms for protection or luck

Biblical warning:

> I will set my face against anyone who turns to mediums and spiritists to prostitute themselves by following them.
> —LEVITICUS 20:6

Such practices attempt to replace God's power with counterfeit forces.

Games and practices disguised as "entertainment"

Seemingly harmless activities that open spiritual doors, including these:

- Ouija boards: marketed as a game, but used to contact spirits

- Light as a Feather, Stiff as a Board: a group levitation game invoking spirits

- Bloody Mary: summoning a spirit through mirrors

- Certain video games or shows with dark occult themes, such as games that require summoning spirits, using spells, or role-playing as a demonic character

Biblical warning:

> Have nothing to do with the fruitless deeds of darkness, but rather expose them.
> —EPHESIANS 5:11

Blood rituals and dark ceremonies

Practices invoking spirits or forces through sacrifice or covenant rituals, including the following:

- Ritualistic animal or blood sacrifices

- Satanic rituals or invocations

- Cutting or binding pacts to summon spiritual power

Biblical warning:

> They sacrificed their sons and their daughters to demons.
> —PSALM 106:37, CEV

God strictly forbids any blood rituals tied to demonic entities or false worship.

Idolatry and worship of false deities

Engaging in rituals to honor or call upon gods other than the true God, such as the following:

- Veneration of idols or objects
- Calling on ancestors or spirits for guidance
- Pagan festivals or celebrations that invoke spiritual entities

Biblical warning:

> You shall have no other gods before me.
>
> —Exodus 20:3

These practices open doors to demonic influence.

What appears to be harmless fun can desensitize participants to spiritual dangers. Beware of any practices that blend spirituality with self-empowerment or enlightenment outside of Christ. These practices often blur the line between self-help and spiritual rebellion against God's truth.

When a demonic portal is opened, the consequences can be severe and far-reaching. These portals allow demonic forces to influence a person, especially in their thoughts and emotions, leading to a downward spiral of spiritual and moral decay. The Bible provides numerous examples of individuals and nations who suffered greatly as a result of opening demonic portals.

One such example is found in the story of Ahab and Jezebel in 1 Kings 16–21. King Ahab, under the influence of his wife, Jezebel, led Israel into idolatry and the worship of Baal. By erecting altars to Baal and engaging in pagan rituals, Ahab opened a demonic portal over the nation of Israel, leading to widespread apostasy and moral corruption. The consequences were devastating, as the nation faced God's judgment in the form of drought and famine.

The prophet Elijah was sent to confront Ahab and Jezebel, calling the people back to the worship of the true God and closing the demonic portal through repentance and a return to righteousness.

The story of Ahab and Jezebel serves as a warning not just to individuals but also to entire societies about the dangers of opening demonic portals. When leaders and nations engage in practices that are abominations before God, they open themselves up to demonic influence on a national scale. This influence can manifest in various ways. A society could experience widespread moral decay, the breakdown of values, and even natural calamities. The Bible often associates such consequences with the judgment of God, as seen in the story of Sodom and Gomorrah, where pervasive wickedness led to the cities' complete destruction and subjection to territorial principalities (Gen. 19).

In the modern context, demonic portals can be opened through the institutionalization of sin—such as the legalization of practices that contradict God's laws. When societies embrace such actions, they effectively invite demonic forces to exert influence over all aspects of the culture—politics, the economy, even the moral fabric of the people. This influence can lead to an increase in crime and corruption (sound familiar?). The role of the church, therefore, is critical in standing up against these forces—both through prayer and spiritual warfare, as well as advocating for righteousness with courage and fortitude.

Recognizing Demonic Portals

Recognizing demonic portals is an essential skill for believers who want to live in spiritual victory. These portals can manifest in various ways, often accompanied by signs of spiritual oppression. Confusion and an impending sense of darkness or doom are quite common. Other indicators of demonic portals include persistent sinful behavior, involvement in occult practices, and exposure to environments or objects that carry spiritual darkness.

The Bible provides guidance on discerning demonic influences. In 1 John 4:1, believers are instructed to "test the spirits to see whether they are from God, because many false prophets have gone out into the world." This testing involves discerning whether the source of influence aligns with God's Word and the teachings of Jesus Christ. If something tempts a person to sin, leading them away from the truth of the gospel and toward deception and darkness, it is likely connected to a demonic portal.

Another biblical principle for discerning demonic portals is found in James 3:15–17, where the apostle James contrasts heavenly wisdom with earthly or even demonic wisdom. He describes demonic wisdom as especially characterized by selfishness and disorder. If a person's life or environment is marked by these negative traits, it may indicate the presence of a demonic portal.

Discerning demonic portals requires a combination of spiritual sensitivity, knowledge of Scripture, and the guidance of the Holy Spirit. As we each develop a deep relationship with God, this intimacy helps to heighten our spiritual discernment. Regular prayer and fasting can equip us to recognize the signs of demonic activity and to respond appropriately.

In addition to personal spiritual practices, seeking counsel from mature believers experienced in spiritual warfare is highly beneficial. These individuals can offer valuable insight and guidance in discerning and addressing demonic portals. Proverbs 11:14 emphasizes the importance of wise counsel: "Where there is no guidance, a people falls, but in an abundance of counselors there is safety" (ESV). By seeking the advice and support of a spiritual community, we can more effectively navigate the challenges posed by demonic influences.

Closing Demonic Portals Through Repentance and Deliverance

Once a demonic portal has been identified, it is crucial to take immediate steps to close it and prevent further spiritual harm. The process of closing a demonic portal involves repentance and clear renunciation. Deliverance sessions may even be necessary.

1. **Repentance and confession:** The first step in closing a demonic portal is to confess and repent of any sin that may have opened the portal. Repentance involves a genuine change of heart and mind, turning away from sin and toward God. Confession brings these sins before God, acknowledging the wrongs done and seeking His forgiveness. James 5:16 emphasizes the power of confession: "Therefore confess your sins to each other and pray for each other so that you may be healed. The prayer of a righteous person is powerful and effective." Through repentance and confession, the legal right that the enemy has to operate in a person's life is removed, beginning the process of closing the portal.

2. **Renunciation:** After repentance, the next step is to renounce any involvement with sinful or occult practices or demonic influences that may have opened the portal. Renunciation is a verbal declaration rejecting and breaking all ties with these practices and influences. An example of this practice can be found in Acts 19:18–19, where new believers in Ephesus who had previously practiced sorcery brought their scrolls together and burned them publicly, renouncing their past involvement in the occult. This step is vital because it severs the

connection between the individual and the forces of darkness, cutting off any further access that demons might have. Renunciation can be done through specific prayers where the individual declares their rejection of any agreements or actions that have given the enemy a foothold. For instance, someone who has been involved in occult practices might pray, "In the name of Jesus, I renounce all involvement with witchcraft, divination, and any other occult practices. I break every tie and agreement with these practices and command all associated spirits to leave my life immediately."

3. **Deliverance:** In some cases, closing a demonic portal may require deliverance, which involves casting out demonic forces that have entered through the portal. Deliverance is a ministry that was central to Jesus' work on earth, as He consistently cast out demons from those who were oppressed. Mark 16:17 records Jesus' declaration: "And these signs will accompany those who believe: In my name they will drive out demons." Deliverance should be carried out by individuals who are equipped and spiritually mature, as it can be a complex process. The authority of Jesus' name holds the power to cast out demons from people, but anyone attempting deliverance should be prayed up in faith, and fasting if possible. The goal of deliverance is to expel any demonic presence and to restore the individual to spiritual wholeness. (We'll look deeper into this subject matter in chapter 9.)

4. **Filling the void with God's presence:** Once the demonic portal has been closed through repentance and clear renunciation (and deliverance, if

necessary), it is essential to fill the void left by the departing demonic forces with the presence of God. This step is crucial because leaving the void empty creates an opportunity for the enemy to return, often with more intensity. Jesus warned of this danger in Matthew 12:43–45: "When an impure spirit comes out of a person, it goes through arid places seeking rest and does not find it. Then it says, 'I will return to the house I left.' When it arrives, it finds the house unoccupied, swept clean and put in order. Then it goes and takes with it seven other spirits more wicked than itself, and they go in and live there. And the final condition of that person is worse than the first." To prevent this relapse, it is vital to fill one's life with the things of God. Pray and read the Bible, and make sure you are involved in a local church where you can worship the Lord with other strong believers.

5. **Ongoing vigilance and spiritual maintenance:** After a demonic portal has been closed, ongoing vigilance is necessary to ensure it remains closed. Holiness is important to God, and the devil knows if we are not living holy lives. Staying close to God and walking in obedience to what He has asked in His Word is absolutely necessary. We also must be mindful of the influences we allow into our lives, avoiding anything that could reopen the portal, whether that be a relationship we need to cut off or a TV show we should not watch. Paul's exhortation in Ephesians 6:10–18 to "put on the full armor of God" (v. 11) is particularly relevant here, as it provides a blueprint for living a life that is protected from demonic influence. The armor of God—truth,

righteousness, the gospel of peace, faith, salvation,
the Word of God, and prayer—serves as both a
defense and an offense against the enemy's schemes.

The church plays a vital role in helping individuals close demonic portals and live in spiritual freedom. As the body of Christ, the church is called to minister deliverance, provide teaching on spiritual warfare, and support believers in their journeys toward holiness and spiritual maturity. The community of believers will pray for you *and* keep you accountable, and that is essential in the process of closing demonic portals and maintaining spiritual victory.

The church's responsibility in spiritual warfare extends beyond individual deliverance. It includes equipping the saints for battle through sound teaching, fostering an environment where the Holy Spirit can work powerfully, and standing in the gap for communities and nations through intercessory prayer. In Ephesians 4:11–13, Paul outlined the roles of apostles, prophets, evangelists, pastors, and teachers within the church: "So Christ himself gave the apostles, the prophets, the evangelists, the pastors and teachers, to equip his people for works of service, so that the body of Christ may be built up until we all reach unity in the faith and in the knowledge of the Son of God and become mature, attaining to the whole measure of the fullness of Christ." This equipping includes teaching believers how to recognize and close demonic portals. Part of this understanding must include how to engage in spiritual warfare effectively and how to live in the victory that Christ has already secured.

The church also plays a critical role in corporate repentance and intercession. Throughout the Bible, we see instances where the collective repentance of God's people leads to the closing of demonic portals and the restoration of God's blessing. In 2 Chronicles 7:14, God gave a powerful promise to His people: "If my people, who are called by my name, will humble themselves and pray and seek my face and turn from their wicked ways, then I will hear from heaven, and I will forgive their sin and will heal their land." This promise highlights the power of collective action in closing demonic portals and bringing about spiritual renewal.

Understanding demonic portals is crucial for believers who seek to live in the fullness of God's protection and blessing. These portals are real and have the potential to cause significant spiritual harm if left unchecked. However, through repentance, renunciation, deliverance, and the ongoing pursuit of holiness, these portals can be closed and the power of the enemy broken.

The church plays a vital role in this process, providing the support, teaching, and spiritual authority needed to help believers recognize and close these portals. As we continue to grow in our understanding of spiritual warfare, let us remain vigilant, always seeking the guidance of the Holy Spirit and standing firm in the victory Christ has already won.

May we live lives that are free from the influence of demonic portals, fully immersed in the presence and protection of God, and equipped to help others experience the same freedom.

Activation Prayer

Heavenly Father, I come before You with humility and gratitude, acknowledging Your sovereignty and power over all things. Thank You for the wisdom and truth revealed in this chapter, equipping me to discern and close demonic portals in my life.

Lord, I repent of any associations I may have had that opened doors to darkness. I ask for Your forgiveness and cleansing by the blood of Jesus. I renounce all ties to sin, especially any occult practices, and I declare that I belong to You alone.

Father, strengthen me with Your Spirit to stand firm against the schemes of the enemy. Surround me with Your heavenly host of angels, and let Your light remove all darkness. Fill every area of my life with Your presence and Your mighty power. Teach me to walk in holiness, obedience, and vigilance so that I may glorify You in all I do.

Lord, I pray for my community and nation. Where demonic portals have been opened, I ask for Your intervention and deliverance. Father, raise up Your church to be a beacon of light and truth, bringing freedom to those in bondage.

In the mighty and victorious name of Jesus Christ, I pray. Amen.

DID YOU KNOW?

Neuroscience has shown that exposure to prolonged fear and negative imagery (as in certain horror media or occult practices) rewires neural pathways, increasing susceptibility to anxiety and spiritual oppression. This connection reinforces the spiritual principle of guarding what you allow into your life.

PORTALS IN POP CULTURE:
The Deliverance (2024 film)

The movie *The Deliverance* is based on the real-life experiences of Latoya Ammons and her family, who claimed that their home in Gary, Indiana, was haunted by demonic forces in 2011. The events included physical attacks, possessions, and inexplicable occurrences, which led many to believe a demonic portal had been opened. Let this story be a reminder: Always be spiritually discerning and sensitive to the environments you step into. Occupy them with authority. Drive out darkness and boldly manifest the light of Christ within you.

CHAPTER 3

THE BATTLE FOR THE SOUL

IN THE SPIRITUAL realm, the battle for the soul is a constant and intense conflict between the forces of good and evil. At the center of this struggle are heavenly and demonic portals, which serve as gateways for divine or demonic influences to enter a person's life. Understanding this battle is crucial for every believer, and that includes you. It will directly impact your relationship with God—even your eternal destiny.

Over nearly two decades of preaching the gospel, I've had the privilege of witnessing countless individuals set free by the power of God. Yet I have also seen the enemy's relentless efforts to destroy souls. Demonic portals, even small openings, can become opportunities for the three things demons love most: oppressing believers, suppressing the will of God in their lives, and, if they can, even possessing human beings to carry out their own agenda in the world.

One encounter stands out vividly in my mind. I was ministering to a young woman who, during the session, suddenly fell to the ground and began moving in a snakelike motion. As I pressed deeper into prayer and placed my hand on her head, her movements intensified. The Holy Spirit instructed me to address the spirit of the snake directly.

When I commanded the snake spirit to leave her, her tongue began to move in a slithering motion, and her eyes rolled back, revealing areas the enemy had targeted. As I prayed, I asked the spirit how it had entered her life. The answers were revealing and sobering.

She admitted she had been surrounded by family members who were deeply involved in the occult. Because they were blood relatives, she struggled to cut ties, despite the negative spiritual influences they brought into her life. The second entry point was through what she consumed with her eyes—social media content laced with occult imagery and themes. Clearly this close involvement with the things of the enemy would open a portal into her life while she was awake. But what she didn't realize was that it also opened the door for her to be tormented at night, in her dreams. Like a true-to-life horror movie, she began to be visited by demonic forces in the night.

As we continued the deliverance session, the young woman renounced her connections to these influences, repenting of what she had allowed into her life. She cut those spiritual ties and turned her heart fully to the Lord Jesus. By His power, she was completely set free. This encounter reinforced the reality of the battle for the soul and the critical importance of guarding every gateway—those senses that God gave us to see, hear, and feel. We must be careful of what we engage with in this world!

The Reality of Spiritual Warfare

Spiritual warfare is a fundamental concept in Christian theology, acknowledging the ongoing battle between the kingdom of God and the kingdom of darkness. The apostle Paul vividly described this battle in Ephesians 6:12, stating, "For our struggle is not against flesh and blood, but against the rulers, against the authorities, against the powers of this dark world and against the spiritual forces of evil in the heavenly realms." This verse highlights the spiritual nature of the conflict. Our true enemy is never another human being. The demonic forces that seek to influence and destroy us are the ones behind the conflicts in our lives.

Heavenly and demonic portals are battlegrounds in this spiritual war. Heavenly portals are opened when we open ourselves to God's presence and power in our lives. In contrast, demonic portals are opened through sin, especially rebellion and dabbling in the occult, giving the enemy access to influence and oppress. The battle for the soul involves closing these demonic portals and keeping heavenly portals open, ensuring that the believer remains under God's protection and blessing.

The reality of spiritual warfare is not just a distant or abstract concept; it is something that believers face daily. Our thoughts and actions can either align with God's kingdom or give the enemy a foothold. This constant battle requires vigilance and discernment, as the enemy often operates in subtle ways. He will deceive us, using temptation and fear to lead us astray. In 2 Corinthians 10:3–5, Paul explained the nature of this warfare: "For though we live in the world, we do not wage war as the world does. The weapons we fight with are not the weapons of the world. On the contrary, they have divine power to demolish strongholds. We demolish arguments and every pretension that sets itself up against the knowledge of God, and we take captive every thought to make it obedient to Christ." This passage underscores the importance of spiritual vigilance and the power of God's Word in overcoming the enemy.

One of the most significant aspects of the battle for the soul is the role of free will. God has given every person the freedom to choose whom they will serve and how they will live their life. This freedom includes the ability to open or close spiritual portals based on one's decisions and actions.

In Deuteronomy 30:19, God presented a choice to the people of Israel: "This day I call the heavens and the earth as witnesses against you that I have set before you life and death, blessings and curses. Now choose life, so that you and your children may live." This choice between life and death, blessings and curses, is a decision that every person must make. Choosing life and obedience to God opens heavenly portals, allowing His blessings to flow, while choosing sin and rebellion opens demonic portals, leading to destruction.

The power of free will is also illustrated in the story of Adam and Eve in the Garden of Eden (Gen. 3). By choosing to disobey

God and eat the forbidden fruit, Adam and Eve opened a demonic portal that allowed sin and death to enter the world. Their decision had far-reaching consequences, affecting not only their lives but also the entire human race. This story serves as a powerful reminder of the importance of making choices that align with God's will, as our decisions can either invite God's blessings or expose us to the enemy's attacks.

Free will is both a gift and a responsibility. It allows individuals to choose their paths in life, but with that choice comes the responsibility to align with God's will. We make decisions every day. Will we forgive or hold a grudge? Will we speak truth or tell a lie? These decisions determine which spiritual portals are opened in our lives. The Bible consistently emphasizes the importance of making righteous choices. In Joshua 24:15, Joshua challenged the Israelites, saying, "But if serving the LORD seems undesirable to you, then choose for yourselves this day whom you will serve, whether the gods your ancestors served beyond the Euphrates, or the gods of the Amorites, in whose land you are living. But as for me and my household, we will serve the LORD." This declaration highlights the power of choice and the impact it has not only on the individual but also on their entire household.

Now let's go deeper into what opening these portals looks like in practice.

The Bible alludes to various portals or "gates," which are entry points through which external influences can affect the soul (mind, will, and emotions). These gates must be guarded to ensure they align with God's truth. Below are the key gates with clear examples and references:

Eye gate (what we see)
The eyes are often described as a gateway to the soul, influencing thoughts, desires, and actions.

The eye is the lamp of the body. If your eyes are healthy, your whole body will be full of light. But if your eyes are unhealthy, your whole body will be full of darkness.

—MATTHEW 6:22–23

Example:
Positive influence: Meditating on Scripture or God's creation

I will set no worthless thing before my eyes.

—PSALM 101:3, NASB

Negative influence: Lust or perversion through visual temptation

From the roof he saw a woman bathing. The woman was very beautiful, and David sent someone to find out about her.

—2 SAMUEL 11:2–3

Ear gate (what we hear)

The ears receive words and sounds that influence our faith, thoughts, and emotions.

Faith comes from hearing, and hearing through the word of Christ.

—ROMANS 10:17, ESV

Do not be misled: "Bad company corrupts good character."

—1 CORINTHIANS 15:33

Example:
Positive influence: Hearing God's Word or uplifting speech

Incline your ear to wisdom, and apply your heart to understanding.

—PROVERBS 2:2, NKJV

Negative influence: Listening to gossip, slander, or false teachings

> Their talk will spread like gangrene.
> —2 TIMOTHY 2:17, ESV

Mouth gate (what we speak)

Our words reflect and impact the state of our souls and others'. The mouth can be a gate through which blessings or curses flow.

> Death and life are in the power of the tongue, and those who love it will eat its fruits.
> —PROVERBS 18:21, ESV

> Out of the abundance of the heart the mouth speaks.
> —MATTHEW 12:34, NKJV

Example:
Positive influence: Speaking blessings, truth, and encouragement

> Let the words of my mouth...be pleasing to you.
> —PSALM 19:14, CEB

Negative influence: Speaking lies, curses, or negativity

> With the tongue we praise our Lord...and with it we curse human beings.
> —JAMES 3:9

Nose gate (what we smell)

While less explicitly mentioned, the Bible uses the sense of smell symbolically to describe spiritual discernment and worship.

> Christ loved us and gave himself up for us, a fragrant offering and sacrifice to God.
> —EPHESIANS 5:2, ESV

Example:
Positive influence: Smelling incense or offerings as acts of worship (scented anointing oil)

> The smoke of the incense, together with the prayers of God's people, went up before God.
>
> —Revelation 8:4

Negative influence: The smell of idolatrous sacrifices

> Then he...defiled the high places where the priests had burned incense.
>
> —2 Kings 23:8, nasb

Touch gate (what we feel or engage with physically)

Physical touch and interaction can evoke spiritual or emotional responses, for good or ill.

> Touch no unclean thing, and I will receive you.
>
> —2 Corinthians 6:17

Example:
Positive influence: Acts of ministry like anointing or laying hands on

> Jesus put out His hand and touched him, saying, "I am willing; be cleansed."
>
> —Matthew 8:3, nkjv

Negative influence: Engaging in sin through physical actions

> The woman saw that the fruit of the tree was good....She took some and ate it.
>
> —Genesis 3:6

Mind gate (what we think)

Thoughts and meditations are gates through which the soul is influenced. Guarding the mind protects the soul from corruption.

> Do not conform to the pattern of this world, but be transformed by the renewing of your mind.
>
> —ROMANS 12:2

> Take captive every thought to make it obedient to Christ.
>
> —2 CORINTHIANS 10:5

Example:
Positive influence: Meditating on Scripture

> Blessed is the one...who meditates on his law day and night.
>
> —PSALM 1:1–2

Negative influence: Dwelling on sinful or fearful thoughts

> But each person is tempted when they are dragged away by their own evil desire and enticed. Then, after desire has conceived, it gives birth to sin; and sin, when it is full-grown, gives birth to death.
>
> —JAMES 1:14–15

Heart gate (what we allow to enter spiritually and emotionally)

The heart represents the core of one's being, influenced by all other gates and determining the state of the soul.

> Above all else, guard your heart, for everything you do flows from it.
>
> —PROVERBS 4:23

Example:
Positive influence: Filling the heart with God's Word and love

I have hidden your word in my heart.
—Psalm 119:11

Negative influence: Allowing unforgiveness, bitterness, or idolatry to take root

Their hearts are always going astray.
—Hebrews 3:10

Here's a quick summary:

- **Eyes:** What you see influences your inner thoughts and desires.

- **Ears:** What you hear affects faith and spiritual discernment.

- **Mouth:** Words reflect and shape the soul.

- **Nose:** Fragrance symbolizes discernment and spiritual offerings.

- **Touch:** Physical actions and interactions impact the soul.

- **Mind:** Thoughts and meditations shape the inner being.

- **Heart:** The heart is the seat of emotions and the spiritual core.

Each gate must be actively guarded and aligned with God's Word to protect the soul from harm and cultivate spiritual growth.

Heavenly and demonic portals have a profound influence on the soul. They can even shape what we think and how we feel, which in turn influences the actions we choose to take. When heavenly portals are open, the soul is nourished by God's presence, leading to spiritual growth, peace, and joy. The influence of these portals can be seen in the fruit of the Spirit, as described in Galatians 5:22–23: "But the fruit of the Spirit is love, joy, peace, forbearance, kindness, goodness, faithfulness, gentleness and self-control." These qualities are evidence of a life that is connected to God through heavenly portals.

On the other hand, when demonic portals are open, the soul becomes vulnerable to darkness and oppression, resulting in negative emotions, destructive behaviors, and spiritual bondage. The Bible warns about the consequences of allowing demonic influences into one's life. In Galatians 5:19–21, Paul has listed the acts of the flesh, which include "sexual immorality, impurity and debauchery; idolatry and witchcraft; hatred, discord, jealousy, fits of rage, selfish ambition, dissensions, factions and envy; drunkenness, orgies, and the like." These behaviors are clear signs that demonic portals are at work, pulling the soul away from God and toward spiritual ruin.

The influence of heavenly and demonic portals has real and tangible effects on a person's life. Those who consistently open heavenly portals through prayer, worship, and obedience to God will experience His peace, guidance, and provision. They will find themselves growing in spiritual maturity, exhibiting the fruit of the Spirit, and being used by God to bless others. Conversely, those who open demonic portals through sin, rebellion, and occult practices will find themselves trapped in a cycle of spiritual darkness and despair. They may struggle with depression, anxiety, addiction, and other forms of bondage that hinder their relationship with God and their ability to live in victory.

The Bible provides numerous examples of individuals who experienced the consequences of opening demonic portals. King Saul's descent into madness and despair after consulting the medium of Endor is one such example (1 Samuel 28). Another is Judas Iscariot, who allowed greed and betrayal to open a demonic portal that led to his ultimate destruction (John 13:27). These stories serve as stark warnings of the dangers of opening demonic portals and the importance of remaining vigilant in our spiritual lives.

How to Discern and Engage in the Battle for the Soul

Engaging in the battle for the soul requires spiritual discernment and a proactive approach to close demonic portals while opening heavenly ones. Discernment is the ability to recognize the spiritual influences at work in one's life and determine whether they are from God or the enemy. In Hebrews 5:14, the writer spoke of mature believers who "by constant use have trained themselves to distinguish good from evil." This level of spiritual maturity is essential for engaging effectively in the battle for the soul.

One of the key tools for discernment is the Word of God. Scripture provides the standard by which all spiritual influences should be judged. In 2 Timothy 3:16–17, Paul wrote, "All Scripture is God-breathed and is useful for teaching, rebuking, correcting and training in righteousness, so that the servant of God may be thoroughly equipped for every good work." By studying and meditating on the Bible, we can develop the discernment needed to recognize when a demonic portal is being opened and take steps to close it.

Prayer is another essential tool in the battle for the soul. Through prayer, we can seek God's guidance, ask for His protection, and intercede on behalf of ourselves and others. Jesus modeled the importance of prayer in spiritual warfare when He taught His disciples to pray, "And lead us not into temptation, but deliver us from the evil one" (Matt. 6:13). This prayer acknowledges the reality of spiritual warfare and the need for God's intervention to protect and guide the soul.

In addition to prayer and the study of Scripture, we should engage in spiritual practices that strengthen our connection to

God and keep heavenly portals open. Worship, fasting, and fellow-ship with other believers are powerful ways to invite God's presence into one's life and to build spiritual resilience. Worship, in particular, is a vital tool in spiritual warfare, as it invites the presence of God and drives away demonic influences.

In 2 Chronicles 20, we see a powerful example of the role of worship in spiritual warfare. King Jehoshaphat and the people of Judah faced a vast and formidable army. Rather than succumbing to fear, Jehoshaphat called for a time of prayer and fasting. He then appointed singers to go ahead of the army, praising God with songs of worship. As they sang "Give thanks to the LORD, for his love endures forever," the Lord set ambushes against the enemy forces, leading to a miraculous victory (vv. 21–22). This account demonstrates how worship can open a heavenly portal, inviting God's intervention in the battle and turning the tide in favor of His people.

Fasting is another powerful practice that sharpens spiritual discernment and strengthens the believer's resolve in spiritual warfare. In the Bible, fasting is often associated with seeking God's guidance, humbling oneself before Him, and gaining spiritual clarity. Jesus Himself fasted for forty days in the wilderness before beginning His public ministry, during which He resisted the temptations of the devil (Matt. 4:1–11). Fasting helps us deny the flesh, heighten our sensitivity to the Holy Spirit, and focus on spiritual matters, making it an effective tool in discerning and closing demonic portals.

Fellowship with other believers also plays a crucial role in spiritual discernment and warfare. The community of faith provides support, accountability, and collective wisdom that can help individuals recognize and address the spiritual influences in their lives. Hebrews 10:24–25 exhorts believers, "And let us consider how we may spur one another on toward love and good deeds, not giving up meeting together, as some are in the habit of doing, but encouraging one another—and all the more as you see the Day approaching." Being part of a vibrant faith community ensures that we are not fighting the battle for the soul in isolation but are strengthened by the prayers and support of others.

The Holy Spirit plays a central role in the battle for the soul, empowering us to resist the enemy and to walk in the fullness of God's grace. In John 16:13, Jesus describes the Holy Spirit as the "Spirit of truth," who guides believers "into all the truth." The Holy Spirit will help you discern things you do not already know or remind you of things you do already know, and He will give you the strength you need to close demonic portals and to open heavenly ones.

One of the ways the Holy Spirit assists in the battle for the soul is by convicting us of sin and leading us to repentance. In John 16:8, Jesus said, "When [the Holy Spirit] comes, he will convict the world concerning sin and righteousness and judgment" (ESV). This conviction is a critical step in closing demonic portals, as it prompts believers to turn away from sin and to seek God's forgiveness and restoration. The Holy Spirit's conviction is not meant to condemn us. He wants to lead each of us to a place of repentance and renewed fellowship with God.

The Holy Spirit's role as a guide and counselor is essential in the battle for the soul. He not only convicts of sin, but He also provides the wisdom and guidance we need to navigate life's challenges and spiritual warfare. In Romans 8:26–27, Paul spoke of the Holy Spirit's intercession on behalf of believers: "In the same way, the Spirit helps us in our weakness. We do not know what we ought to pray for, but the Spirit himself intercedes for us through wordless groans. And he who searches our hearts knows the mind of the Spirit, because the Spirit intercedes for God's people in accordance with the will of God." The Holy Spirit's intercession is a powerful resource in spiritual warfare, as He prays according to God's will, aligning our prayers with the purposes of heaven.

The Holy Spirit also equips us with spiritual gifts that are essential for spiritual warfare. In 1 Corinthians 12:7–11, Paul has listed several gifts of the Spirit, some of which are especially helpful in combating the enemy. Wisdom and knowledge, along with discernment of spirits, help us identify his schemes. Faith, healing, and miraculous powers then help us overcome him. These gifts enable believers to engage effectively in the battle for the soul, providing us with the supernatural resources needed to overcome the enemy. The gift of discernment of spirits, in particular, is vital in identifying the presence and influence of demonic portals, allowing believers to take appropriate action to close them.

Moreover, the Holy Spirit empowers believers to live victorious lives by filling us with God's presence and power. In Acts 1:8, Jesus promised His disciples, "But you will receive power when the Holy Spirit comes on you; and you will be my witnesses in Jerusalem, and in all Judea and Samaria, and to the ends of the earth." Many of us understand this verse to apply to witnessing to other people, but did you know it's also for overcoming the challenges and temptations we face in this life? The Holy Spirit's empowerment enables us to overcome sin as we resist the enemy and then live in the victory that Jesus secured through His death, resurrection, and ascension.

Living in the victory of the Holy Spirit involves a daily reliance on Him, inviting His presence into our everyday lives. It requires an intentional surrender to His leading, allowing Him to shape us in everything we do. As we yield to the Holy Spirit, we find that the fruit of the Spirit—love, joy, peace, forbearance, kindness, goodness, faithfulness, gentleness, and self-control—becomes increasingly evident in our lives (Gal. 5:22–23). These qualities not only reflect a life connected to God, but they also serve as a powerful defense against the enemy's attacks.

The Holy Spirit also plays a crucial role in transforming the mind, which is a key battleground in the fight for the soul. Romans 12:2 urges believers, "Do not conform to the pattern of this world, but be transformed by the renewing of your mind. Then you will be able to test and approve what God's will is—his good, pleasing and perfect will." The Holy Spirit renews the mind by replacing worldly patterns of thinking with God's truth, enabling believers to discern and follow God's will. This transformation is essential in closing demonic portals, as it aligns our thoughts with the mind of Christ and prevents the enemy from gaining a foothold.

The battle for the soul is a dynamic and ongoing battle that requires us to stay vigilant. We need the help of the Holy Spirit as well. Heavenly and demonic portals lie at the heart of this conflict, serving as gateways through which divine or demonic influences can enter a person's life. We must first understand the reality of spiritual warfare and then engage in spiritual practices that open heavenly portals. When we do, we can live in the victory that Christ has secured for us.

The Holy Spirit plays a vital role in this battle. He convicts us of any sin in our lives, but He also guides us and empowers us to resist the enemy while walking in the fullness of God's grace. As we cultivate a deep relationship with the Holy Spirit, we are equipped first to discern and close demonic portals and then to keep heavenly portals open. When we do this, we can live in the victory that comes from being aligned with God's will.

May we all remain steadfast in the battle for the soul, relying on the Holy Spirit's power and guidance and standing firm in the victory that is ours in Christ Jesus.

Activation Prayer

Heavenly Father, I worship and adore You. I thank You for filling me with the presence and power of the Holy Spirit, as well as granting me the spiritual armor I need to stand against the schemes of the enemy.

Lord, I ask for discernment to recognize and close any demonic portals that may have been opened in my life. I renounce and reject every influence that does not align with Your truth, and I declare that my heart, mind, and soul belong to You alone. Help me guard the gates of my soul—my eyes, ears, thoughts, and words—so that I remain pure and set apart for Your purposes.

Holy Spirit, guide me daily and empower me to walk in victory. Strengthen me to resist temptation and to stand firm in my faith. Let Your light shine through me as a testimony of Your grace and power.

I declare that no weapon formed against me shall prosper and that I am more than a conqueror through Christ Jesus. Thank You, Lord, for the victory that is already mine through Your Son. May I continue to seek You, trust You, and rely on Your strength as I engage in this battle.

In the mighty name of Jesus, I pray. Amen.

DID YOU KNOW?

Research on neuroplasticity demonstrates that intentional thoughts can rewire the brain. This research aligns with the spiritual principle that renewing your mind is a powerful tool in battling spiritual forces and aligning with heavenly realities (Rom. 12:2).

PORTALS IN POP CULTURE:
Music Festival Tragedy (November 5, 2021)

During a famous rapper's concert in Houston, eight people died, and many attendees reported a dark, oppressive atmosphere. Symbolism in the stage design—featuring a large, fiery portal and eerie imagery—sparked theories that the event was linked to spiritual darkness. Social media exploded with claims that the concert represented a "demonic portal." This tragedy is a sobering reminder: There are places and spaces believers should never step into. More than ever, this moment calls us to cry out to God in humility for mercy, protection, and divine intervention for our generation.

CHAPTER 4

OPENING HEAVENLY PORTALS THROUGH PRAYER

Much has been said about prayer. The sheer number of conferences, seminars, and volumes of literature dedicated to the subject is staggering. While I don't intend to rehash what has already been thoroughly explored, I do believe it is important to review some foundational concepts of prayer as we journey together. However, my goal is to take us deeper—beyond the surface level—into the profound spiritual dimensions of prayer connected to portals.

Prayer is more than a religious activity or discipline, although sometimes we treat it like that is all it is. But no, prayer is powerful! It is a *divine* communication channel that bridges the natural and supernatural realms! When a person aligns with the frequency of prayer, a spiritual opening occurs, creating access to heavenly realities.

Our Master, the Lord Jesus, fully understood this truth. His life of prayer was so compelling and transformative that it prompted His disciples to seek specific instruction on the subject (Luke 11). Of all the things they could have asked Him to teach, they chose to learn the depths of prayer. This request led to the famous Lord's Prayer, which, contrary to common practice, was never meant to be recited as a mere religious formula. When treated as a habitual incantation, its words lose their transformative power. However, when the spirit of the prayer is truly understood, it sparks a spiritual revolution in the believer's mind and heart.

Take, for instance, the declaration "Your kingdom come, your will be done, on earth as it is in heaven" (Matt. 6:10). These words unveil a profound truth: Earth—all of creation, including humanity—was always meant to experience the reality of heaven. This prayer was not a mere wish but a revelation of divine intent, reminding us of God's original design. The Messiah's ultimate mission was to restore that reality.

Eden, the paradise of humanity's beginning, exemplified this heavenly reality. Eden represented fullness and glory. It's where human beings experienced God's very presence, His light, His dominion, and His authority in all its fullness. It is where they lived life in perfect harmony with God. However, the fall of Adam and Eve disrupted this divine design. Christ, as the "Second Adam" (Rom. 5:12–21; 1 Cor. 15:22, 44–49; cf. Eph. 1:10), came to reconcile us back to that original revelation of Eden—a place where heaven meets earth.

Through prayer, we are invited to align with this eternal truth. We can't treat prayer as a mechanism to get our requests answered, not when it is the spiritual conduit through which we access the very reality of God's kingdom! Prayer allows heaven to invade the earth—both within us and around us. This is the transformative power of prayer, as taught and exemplified by our Savior.

The Lord instructed me to enter into a time of prayer and fasting. What I intended to be just a few hours in the church sanctuary, seeking His presence, transformed into an overnight encounter with the Holy Spirit. There was a pressing in my spirit, a sense that the Lord had more to reveal; so I lingered, determined to remain until He spoke.

As I continued to pray, I entered a deep state of intercession and a visionary trance. In this vision, I found myself walking into a familiar space—a hotel room where our church had previously held services. As I entered, I was greeted by a figure who appeared to be a general of God, someone I recognized from my earthly life but whose brilliance and presence revealed that he was not merely human. I discerned that this was a divine representation, an angelic being sent for a specific purpose.

Without speaking, he gestured for me to follow. As we walked through a hallway, I saw others waiting—two mighty generals of God who had gone on to glory, and one woman of God who had left an enduring legacy of faith. Their lives had been marked by a holy anointing that brought miracles down from heaven. These were individuals whose ministries had shaken the nations. They had advanced God's kingdom powerfully.

The general led me to the center of a semicircle formed by these great people of faith. With every step closer, I felt an overwhelming sense of reverence, humility, and brokenness in my soul. As I knelt in the center, I kept my face to the ground, overwhelmed by the holiness of the moment. Each of them approached in turn, laying their hands on me. With every touch, I felt a transmission of light and power flowing into me. It was an impartation of the divine.

When I returned to my natural state, I knew that the Lord had revealed the next phase of my ministry. This encounter was an undeniable empowerment for the work ahead—a divine confirmation of the call to serve His kingdom in a greater capacity.

How incredible that an unusual time separated in prayer led to such an encounter! Let's go deeper, as I believe that now is a prophetic season where you're leaning into the Holy Spirit like never before. Unforgettable and life-changing encounters await you.

Prayer is one of the most powerful tools a believer has in opening heavenly portals. It is the means by which we communicate with God. Prayer helps us align our hearts with His will, because it is in the midst of His presence and power that we are transformed. Through prayer, we can access the resources of heaven. God divinely intervenes, and His kingdom invades the earth, just as it is in done in heaven. This chapter explores the profound impact of prayer in opening heavenly portals. If you've ever struggled with cultivating a prayer life that ushers in God's presence, read on.

The Power of Prayer in the Spiritual Realm

Many Christians aren't sure of how to pray. They still think of prayer as a religious ritual they "ought" to do more. They have not yet grasped the reality that it is a dynamic interaction with the Creator of the universe! When we pray, we are engaging with the spiritual realm, connecting with God, and inviting His influence into our lives and circumstances. The Bible is filled with examples of how prayer opens heavenly portals, bringing all of the blessings of the Lord down and into our lives in a very practical way.

One of the most dramatic examples of prayer opening a heavenly portal is found in the story of Elijah on Mount Carmel (1 Kings 18:36–39). Elijah, a prophet of God, was in a confrontation with the prophets of Baal to demonstrate who the true God was. After the prophets of Baal failed to call down fire from heaven, Elijah prayed a simple but powerful prayer: "LORD, the God of Abraham, Isaac and Israel, let it be known today that you are God in Israel and that I am your servant and have done all these things at your command. Answer me, LORD, answer me, so these people will know that you, LORD, are God, and that you are turning their hearts back again" (vv. 36–37).

In response to Elijah's prayer, God opened a heavenly portal and sent fire from heaven, consuming the sacrifice, the wood, the stones, and even the water in the trench. The people fell prostrate and declared, "The LORD—he is God! The LORD—he is God!" (v. 39). This story demonstrates the power of prayer to open a heavenly portal, bringing God's miraculous intervention and turning the hearts of the people back to Him.

Yet prayer is not limited to dramatic displays of power like those Elijah experienced. It also opens heavenly portals in the everyday situations of our lives. In the New Testament, the apostle Paul encourages believers to "pray in the Spirit on all occasions with all kinds of prayers and requests" (Eph. 6:18). This instruction highlights the importance of continual, Spirit-led prayer as a way to keep heavenly portals open in our lives, allowing God's presence and power to flow in every circumstance.

Prayer acts as a spiritual defense mechanism, creating a shield around the believer and blocking the enemy's attempts to gain access through demonic portals. When we pray, we are engaging in spiritual warfare, reinforcing the barriers against darkness and opening pathways for God's light and truth to penetrate our lives. In Matthew 26:41, Jesus admonished His disciples, "Watch and pray so that you will not fall into temptation. The spirit is willing, but the flesh is weak." This verse underscores the necessity of prayer in maintaining spiritual vigilance and preventing the enemy from exploiting human weaknesses.

Types of Prayer That Open Heavenly Portals

Different types of prayer can effectively bring down the blessings of God, and they each have a unique focus and impact. Understanding these different types of prayer can help us engage more effectively in our spiritual walk and see greater manifestations of God's presence in our lives.

Intercessory prayer

Intercession involves praying on behalf of others, standing in the gap, and seeking God's intervention in their lives. Through intercessory prayer, heavenly portals can be opened. What do you or your family, community, or nation need? Protection? Healing? The answer to a challenging relationship situation? Deliverance from addiction? As you intercede for others, these and many other breakthroughs can take place! A powerful example of intercession is seen in the Bible with Moses. When the Israelites sinned by worshipping the golden calf, Moses interceded on their behalf. He pleaded with God to forgive their sin and spare them from destruction. In a beautiful answer to prayer, his intercession opened a heavenly portal of mercy, and God relented from the disaster He had planned (Exod. 32:11–14).

Intercessory prayer is often characterized by persistence and fervency. The story of Moses interceding for Israel is one of many examples where persistent prayer made a difference in the spiritual realm. Another powerful example is found in the life of the prophet Daniel. For twenty-one days, Daniel prayed and fasted, seeking understanding and intervention from God concerning a vision he had received. His persistence in prayer opened a heavenly portal, prompting an angel to be dispatched with the answer to his prayers. However, the angel encountered resistance from a demonic principality, the "prince of the Persian kingdom," and was delayed until the archangel Michael came to assist (Dan. 10:12–14). This story illustrates the reality of spiritual warfare in the heavenly realms and the importance of perseverance in intercessory prayer.

Worship and adoration

Worship is a form of prayer that focuses on adoring and praising God for who He is. Worship creates an atmosphere that invites God's presence and opens heavenly portals for divine encounters. In Acts 16, Paul and Silas were imprisoned, yet they prayed and sang hymns to God. As they worshipped, a heavenly portal was opened, and an earthquake shook the prison, opening the doors and breaking their chains (vv. 25–26). Worship invites God's presence, and God's presence *always* brings freedom and breakthrough!

Worship is not only an act of adoration but also a powerful weapon in spiritual warfare. When believers engage in worship, they are declaring the sovereignty and goodness of God, even in the midst of trials. This declaration of faith creates an environment where God's presence can manifest powerfully, dispelling darkness and breaking spiritual chains. The story of Jehoshaphat in 2 Chronicles 20 provides another example of worship as a tool in spiritual warfare. When faced with a vast army, Jehoshaphat appointed singers to go ahead of his troops, singing praises to the Lord. As they worshipped, the Lord set ambushes against the enemy, leading to their defeat without a single weapon being drawn by the Israelites (vv. 21–24). This account demonstrates that worship can open a heavenly portal that brings about divine intervention and victory.

Petition and supplication

Petition is the act of making specific requests to God. When you ask for His help, whether you are praying for a new job or His intervention in a particular situation, you are petitioning Him. Supplication is somewhat different. It involves earnest, humble requests, often accompanied by fasting or deep emotional pleading. Jesus taught His disciples to ask, seek, and knock, promising that those who do so will receive, find, and have doors opened to them (Matt. 7:7–8). Petition and supplication open portals that allow God's blessings to flow by inviting His involvement in the details of our lives and expressing our dependence on Him.

Supplication is a powerful form of prayer that moves the heart of God, especially when offered with sincerity and intensity. The Bible records numerous instances where fervent supplication led to miraculous results. A significant example is the story of Hannah, the mother of the prophet Samuel. Stricken with grief over her barrenness, Hannah went to the temple and poured out her heart to God in supplication. She wept bitterly and made a vow, promising that if God blessed her with a son, she would dedicate him to His service. God heard her supplication and opened a heavenly portal of blessing, resulting in the birth of Samuel, who would become one of Israel's greatest prophets (1 Sam. 1:10–20). Hannah's story illustrates that heartfelt supplication can open portals to heaven. When we pray with honesty and humility from the heart, we can receive God's favor and miraculous intervention.

Prayer of agreement

The prayer of agreement involves two or more people coming together in unity to pray for a specific need or purpose. Jesus emphasized the power of agreement in prayer when He said,

"Again, truly I tell you that if two of you on earth agree about anything they ask for, it will be done for them by my Father in heaven. For where two or three gather in my name, there am I with them" (Matt. 18:19–20). This type of prayer opens us up to the blessings of the Lord by aligning the hearts of believers with each other and with God's will, releasing His power into the situation.

The prayer of agreement leverages the power of unity in the body of Christ. When believers come together in agreement, their collective faith and petition can create a spiritual synergy that opens heavenly portals in ways that individual prayer might not achieve. The early church experienced this power in Acts 12 when Peter was imprisoned. The church gathered together to pray fervently for his release. In response to their united prayers, an angel was sent to free Peter from prison, opening the iron gate that led to the city (vv. 5–10). This miraculous deliverance underscores the power of corporate prayer in opening heavenly portals and bringing about divine intervention.

Practical Steps to Cultivate a Prayer Life That Opens Heavenly Portals

Receiving the benefits of prayer consistently doesn't just happen by default or happenstance. It is essential to develop a disciplined and intentional prayer life. The following practical steps can help each of us cultivate a powerful and effective prayer life:

- **Set a regular prayer time:** Establishing a regular time for prayer each day helps create a habit of seeking God's presence. You can do it anytime, day or night, but setting aside dedicated time for prayer ensures a close connection with God that brings forth His blessings. Daniel, for instance, was known for his disciplined prayer life. Despite the threat of persecution, he prayed three times a day, kneeling before God and giving thanks (Dan. 6:10). His commitment to regular prayer not only sustained his relationship with God but also opened heavenly portals that protected him from his enemies and allowed him to prosper in a foreign land.

• **Create a sacred space:** Setting aside a dedicated space for prayer, free from distractions, can greatly enhance your focus and sense of reverence. This space can be as simple as a corner in your home, a prayer closet, or even a quiet spot outdoors. Having a sacred space can help you enter God's presence more fully and more effectively open your life to His blessings. Jesus often withdrew to solitary places to pray (Luke 5:16). "But Jesus often withdrew to lonely places and prayed." By creating a sacred space, you can cultivate an environment where you can commune with God intimately and experience His presence without interruption.

• **Incorporate Scripture into your prayers:** Praying God's Word is a powerful way to align your prayers with His will. The Bible is filled with promises and declarations that can be used in prayer to align yourself to receive His favor and blessings. For example, when praying for protection, you can declare Psalm 91:1–2: "Whoever dwells in the shelter of the Most High will rest in the shadow of the Almighty. I will say of the LORD, 'He is my refuge and my fortress, my God, in whom I trust.'" Praying Scripture builds faith and invites God's promises to manifest in your life. Jesus Himself used Scripture in His prayers and declarations, particularly when resisting the devil's temptations in the wilderness (Matt. 4:1–11). By incorporating Scripture into your prayers, you tap in to the authority of God's Word, ensuring that your prayers are grounded in truth and power.

- **Engage in fasting:** Fasting, combined with prayer, is a powerful spiritual discipline that opens heavenly portals. Fasting humbles us like nothing else can. It increases our spiritual sensitivity, and that, in turn, intensifies the effectiveness of our prayers. In Mark 9:29, Jesus emphasized the importance of fasting when dealing with certain spiritual challenges, indicating that sometimes divine intervention comes only through prayer and fasting. Fasting creates a heightened awareness of God's presence and aligns the believer's spirit with the Holy Spirit, making it easier to hear God's voice and discern His will. Throughout Scripture, fasting is associated with seeking God and experiencing significant spiritual encounters. For example, before beginning His public ministry, Jesus fasted for forty days and nights, opening a heavenly portal that empowered Him for the challenges ahead (Matt. 4:2). Fasting is also used when people are repenting before the Lord for sin or fervently praying for God to intervene in a desperate situation.

- **Pray with persistence and faith:** Jesus emphasized the importance of persistence in prayer through the parable of the persistent widow (Luke 18:1–8). The widow's relentless pursuit of justice led to her receiving what she desired. Similarly, persistent prayer opens heavenly portals by demonstrating faith and trust in God's ability to answer. James 1:6 encourages believers to pray with faith, not doubting, as doubt can hinder the effectiveness of prayer. Persistence in prayer is an act of spiritual endurance, reflecting a deep-seated belief that God hears and responds to the cries of His people. Elijah's prayer for rain in 1 Kings 18:41–45 is an example of persistent prayer. After praying seven times, Elijah finally saw the small cloud that would bring the end of a long drought. His persistence in prayer opened a heavenly portal that released rain upon the land, demonstrating the power of unwavering faith.

Praise is an often overlooked but incredibly powerful form of prayer. When believers praise God, they acknowledge His greatness, goodness, and sovereignty, which invites His presence into their circumstances. Psalm 22:3 declares, "But You are holy, enthroned in the praises of Israel" (NKJV). This verse indicates that praise creates a throne room where God's presence can dwell.

As we saw previously in the story of King Jehoshaphat in 2 Chronicles 20, praise can open a heavenly portal that brings about divine intervention and victory.

Throughout history, there have been countless testimonies of individuals and communities experiencing the power of God through open heavenly portals as a result of prayer. These testimonies serve as reminders of the effectiveness of prayer and encourage us to continue seeking God with all our hearts.

The Welsh Revival (1904–1905): One such testimony comes from the story of the Welsh Revival of 1904–1905. This revival was marked by intense prayer and worship, which opened heavenly portals over Wales, leading to a powerful outpouring of the Holy Spirit. Thousands of people were saved, churches were filled, and the moral climate of the nation was transformed. The revival was sparked by the prayers of individuals like Evan Roberts, who spent hours in intercession, asking God to send revival to Wales. His prayers opened a heavenly portal that changed the course of history for an entire nation. The Welsh Revival is a testament to how sustained, fervent prayer can open heavenly portals on a large scale, bringing about national transformation and spiritual awakening.

George Müller's Orphanages: Another powerful testimony is that of George Müller, a Christian evangelist and the founder of orphanages in England. Müller was known for his unwavering faith and his commitment to prayer. He prayed daily for the needs of the orphanages, trusting God to provide without ever asking for donations. Over the course of his life, Müller's prayers opened heavenly portals that brought in millions of dollars in today's currency, providing for thousands of orphans without a single appeal for funds. His life is a testament to the power of prayer to open heavenly portals and to bring God's provision in miraculous ways. Müller's testimony demonstrates that we can witness extraordinary provisions and blessings that defy human understanding when we place our trust in God through prayer.

The Azusa Street Revival (1906): The Azusa Street Revival, which began in 1906 in Los Angeles, is another important example of heavenly portals being opened through prayer. Led by William J. Seymour, this revival was characterized by fervent prayer and worship. The manifestation of spiritual gifts was powerful in the meetings, particularly speaking in tongues. As a result, a heavenly portal was opened that led to a significant outpouring of the Holy Spirit, which gave birth to the modern Pentecostal movement. The Azusa Street Revival not only impacted the local community but also had a global influence, spreading the demonstration, power, and work of the Holy Spirit to nations across the world. This revival serves as a reminder that prayer can open the windows of heaven and bring about widespread spiritual renewal and transformation.

The testimonies of revivals like those in Wales and Azusa Street highlight the power of collective prayer in corporate worship. When communities of believers come together in unified prayer and worship, they create an environment where God's presence is welcome, leading to significant miracles taking place in the people's lives. Corporate prayer brings together the faith, passion, and spiritual hunger of many individuals, creating a cumulative effect that can result in a powerful move of God.

The early church experienced this dynamic in Acts 2, where the disciples were gathered together in prayer and worship on the day of Pentecost. "Suddenly a sound like the blowing of a violent wind came from heaven and filled the whole house where they were sitting. They saw what seemed to be tongues of fire that separated and came to rest on each of them. All of them were filled with the Holy Spirit" (vv. 1–4). This event marked the birth of the church and the beginning of a global movement, demonstrating that collective prayer and worship can open heavenly portals that bring about transformative encounters with God.

Activation Prayer

Heavenly Father, I thank You for the gift of prayer, the divine connection that allows me to commune with You and experience Your presence. Lord, teach me to pray continually with fervency and persistence, that I might open heavenly portals and see Your kingdom come on earth as it is in heaven.

Father, empower me to stand firm in spiritual warfare. I commit to turn from distractions as I remain steadfast in my pursuit of You. Let my prayers be guided by Your Holy Spirit, as I speak the promises found in Your Word.

I ask that You open the windows of heaven over my life and all those in my circle of influence. Let Your glory descend, bringing Your powerful transformation into people's lives. May my prayer be pleasing to You and effective in advancing Your kingdom.

In the mighty name of Jesus, I pray. Amen.

DID YOU KNOW?

Studies on meditation and prayer reveal that they activate the brain's default mode network (DMN), enhancing focus and reducing stress. Scientists have noted that deep prayer changes brain activity, fostering peace and spiritual openness—similar to how prayer opens heavenly portals.

PORTALS IN POP CULTURE:
The Bridge Between Worlds in *Thor* (2011 film)

The Bifröst Bridge in the Marvel Cinematic Universe is a portal linking the realms of Asgard and Earth. This depiction of cosmic connectivity resonates with the spiritual idea of heavenly portals providing access to divine power and presence. Unlike fiction, the true bridge between heaven and earth is prayer, which is our divine access point to God's presence and purpose. As this book reveals, when we pray, we don't imagine portals; we spiritually open them.

CHAPTER 5

WORSHIP AS A GATEWAY TO THE DIVINE

NOT LONG AFTER my personal encounter where I perceived the heavens opening over our church (see chapter 2), the Lord confirmed His presence in a public and extraordinary way during one of our Sunday services. At that point, no one knew about my secret time of shut-in prayer and the encounter I had experienced. The Lord, however, had chosen to reveal openly what He had done privately as a sign of His glory and faithfulness.

It began as a normal Sunday service, but as we entered into worship, the atmosphere shifted dramatically. The tangible presence of God filled the room so powerfully that people began to weep and cry out to Him. Without an invitation or a call, individuals rushed to the altar, falling to their knees in repentance and worship. All throughout the sanctuary, people prostrated before God, overwhelmed by His glory.

I remember standing on the platform, unable to move. I felt as though if I stepped in any direction, I might miss what God was doing at that moment. The service came to a complete halt not by human design but by the sovereignty of the Holy Spirit. The weight of His presence was so intense that it felt like a heavy blanket in the air. I fell to my knees and joined the congregation in worship, fully surrendered to His divine work.

During this supernatural encounter, testimonies of healing and deliverance were rampant, and a renewed sense of calling upon the people began to emerge. Many were touched in profound and life-changing ways. One member of our congregation, led by the

Spirit, felt compelled to document the moment with her phone, not knowing the magnitude of what she would later see.

After the service, she shared the photos and video she had taken, and what we saw left us in awe. Visible throughout the sanctuary were radiant, light-filled figures. One figure appeared near me on the stage, seemingly also kneeling and bowing in worship (similar to what is found in Revelation 7:11–12). Others were scattered across the room, each glowing with a distinct, heavenly brilliance.

As someone with experience in photography and videography, I was initially skeptical. I wanted to ensure the images were genuine and not the result of a camera glitch or manipulation. To ensure their authenticity, I consulted three separate professionals to analyze the photos. Each confirmed that the images were genuine and showed no signs of manipulation or camera error.

It became clear to all of us that the Lord had visited us and that the heavens had indeed opened over our church. This encounter was a confirmation of what God had revealed to me in secret—a divine portal to the heavenlies, manifesting His glory for all to see.

These kinds of encounters cause long-lasting transformation. None of us in my family or my entire congregation was the same after that encounter.

Intimacy produces conception, which brings forth birthing. There was a spiritual birthing that took place in which calls were revived, ministries were activated, and many people were healed. The effects of that encounter lasted for years. When the volume of worship is raised, we can't hear anything else, especially not the voices of fear or worry. They are silenced in the presence of the Lord!

In the Gospels, there was a profound worship encounter in which the woman of Luke chapter 7 experienced a glorious and transformative time in worship. Scripture recounts in verses 37–38: "And behold, a woman in the city who was a sinner, when she knew that Jesus sat at the table in the Pharisee's house, brought an alabaster flask of fragrant oil, and stood at His feet behind Him weeping; and she began to wash His feet with her tears, and wiped them with the hair of her head; and she kissed His feet and anointed them with the fragrant oil" (NKJV).

This worship encounter profoundly transformed the woman in Luke 7:37–47, demonstrating how genuine repentance and extravagant love draw us into the depths of Christ's grace. Her actions—anointing Jesus' feet with perfume and tears and wiping them with her hair—were acts of humility and devotion that reflected her deep awareness of her sin and her need for forgiveness. Jesus' response, "Your sins are forgiven" (v. 48, NKJV), not only assured her of her redemption but also restored her identity, lifting her from shame to honor.

From a theological perspective, this encounter illustrates the transformative power of grace. Jesus' parable (vv. 41–43) shows that those who recognize the weight of their sin experience a greater capacity for love when forgiven. The woman's worship wasn't transactional; rather, it was a response to the unmerited favor she received. By forgiving her, Jesus affirmed her dignity and gave her a place in the narrative of salvation history!

Her legacy is remembered as an example of true worship and faith, transcending societal scorn and revealing the heart of the gospel: that forgiveness is not earned but freely given. As Jesus declared in Matthew 26:13, "Wherever this gospel is preached throughout the world, what she has done will also be told, in memory of her." Her story continues to inspire, showing that anyone can approach Jesus with bold faith and be forever transformed by His love. Her worship caused the heavens to open. Can you imagine what your worship can cause in the realm of the Spirit?

Worship That Produces God's Glory

As I often say, worship reveals "worth-ship." To truly understand the transformative power of God's glory, we must first gain a deeper understanding of what sincere and true spiritual worship accomplishes. Let's take a moment to delve deeper into the meaning of *glory.* By comprehending the worthiness of God, we can better grasp the magnitude of the worship He is so deserving of.

The concept of glory in the Bible is rich, multidimensional, and deeply rooted in both the Hebrew and Greek languages. Understanding the original meanings from Hebrew, Greek, and Aramaic sheds light on its theological, spiritual, and symbolic significance in both the Old and New Testaments.

Primary Hebrew word for *glory*: (*kabod*)

The word *kabod* is rooted in the concept of "weight" or "heaviness." In ancient Israel, weight signified value, substance, and importance. For example, a person's wealth or something's value was often measured by its weight (e.g., gold or silver).

- **Symbolic significance:** *Kabod* also appears in contexts of God's manifest presence, especially in the tabernacle and the temple. For example, in Exodus 24:16–17, the glory of the Lord rested upon Mount Sinai, symbolizing God's tangible presence and His relationship with His people. The physical manifestation of God's glory (like a cloud or fire) signified His holiness. His rule is sovereign.

- **Spiritual significance:** *Kabod* implies the worthiness, majesty, honor, and splendor associated with God's presence. It represents the idea that God's presence is so substantial and significant that it "weighs down" on His people with awe and reverence.

Primary Greek word for *glory*: δόξα (*doxa*)

The Greek word *doxa* comes from the root meaning "to seem" or "to appear." In classical Greek, it referred to a person's reputation or honor, but in the New Testament, it takes on a much deeper meaning, indicating God's intrinsic worth and radiance.

In the New Testament, *doxa* represents the honor, majesty, and perfection of God, often expressed through His works and character. It's a reflection of God's true nature. For example, in John 1:14, "We have seen his glory, the glory of the one and only Son," *doxa* describes the manifest presence of God in Jesus Christ. The glory of Jesus reflects the fullness of God and His saving power.

Doxa in the New Testament symbolizes divine light. It is the majesty that comes when God's presence is revealed to humanity. This is seen in the transfiguration (Matt. 17:2), where Jesus' face shone like the sun, symbolizing divine revelation and God's authority over all creation. This idea is further emphasized in the concept of the "hope of glory" (Col. 1:27), where believers anticipate sharing in God's eternal glory.

- **God's manifest presence:** In both the Old and New Testaments, *glory* often denotes God's physical presence. In the Old Testament, His glory filled the tabernacle and the temple, signifying His dwelling among His people (Exod. 40:34–35). In the New Testament, Jesus Himself is described as the manifestation of God's glory (Heb. 1:3), emphasizing that Jesus is the ultimate revelation of God to humanity.

- **Glory as transformation:** For believers, the concept of glory implies a transformative process. In 2 Corinthians 3:18, Paul spoke of us being "transformed into the same image from one degree of glory to another" (ESV). This suggests that as we grow closer to God, we reflect His glory more fully, symbolizing spiritual growth and maturity.

- **The glory of resurrection and eternity:** Glory also signifies the ultimate victory and the hope of resurrection. In Romans 8:18, Paul speaks of "the glory that will be revealed in us," referring to the future, eternal state of believers in God's presence. This glory represents the promise of eternal life and restoration, a hope for all Christians.

- **Worship and praise:** Glory is not only an attribute of God; it is also the purpose of creation's response to Him. Psalm 29:2 encourages worshippers to "ascribe to the LORD the glory due his name." Here, giving glory is an act of acknowledging God's magnificence and authority.

The biblical concept of glory speaks to the essence of God's character, His visible presence, and the way He manifests Himself in the world. It invites believers to respond in worship. When we do, we reflect His nature to others in the here and now, and we look forward to sharing in His glory for eternity. This idea of glory, from *kabod* to *doxa*, reveals the weight and worth of the worship that belongs to God alone.

Now that you have that powerful breakdown, let's go deeper into the practical, experiential side of worship.

Worship is much more than just singing songs or playing music; it is a powerful spiritual practice that opens the gates of heaven, inviting God's presence into our midst. When we engage in true worship, we create an atmosphere where heavenly portals can be opened, allowing divine encounters, healing, deliverance, and revelation to flow. This chapter explores the transformative power of worship as a gateway to the divine and how it can open heavenly portals in our lives.

The Essence of True Worship

Worship is, at its core, an act of reverence and adoration directed toward God. It is an expression of our love, gratitude, and awe for who God is and what He has done. True worship is not limited to a specific style or setting. It is a heart posture that acknowledges God's greatness and gives Him the honor He deserves. In John

4:23–24, Jesus explained the nature of true worship: "Yet a time is coming and has now come when the true worshipers will worship the Father in the Spirit and in truth, for they are the kind of worshipers the Father seeks. God is spirit, and his worshipers must worship in the Spirit and in truth."

Worship in the Spirit and in truth goes beyond external rituals or performances. It is a deep, personal connection with God that flows from a sincere heart. This kind of worship opens heavenly portals because it aligns the worshipper's spirit with the Spirit of God, creating a direct connection between heaven and earth. When we worship in the Spirit and in truth, we are not merely going through the motions; we are entering God's presence, where anything is possible.

True worship is not confined to moments of corporate singing or Sunday services; it is a lifestyle. The gospel exhorts in Mark 12:30, "'And you shall love the LORD your God with all your heart, with all your soul, with all your mind, and with all your strength.' This is the first commandment" (NKJV). This verse highlights that worship is about offering our entire lives—everything we do and say—as an ongoing act of devotion to God. This continuous act of worship keeps the portals of heaven open, allowing God's presence to flow into every aspect of our lives, not just during designated worship times.

Few examples of heavenly portals are as dramatic as Moses' encounters with God on Mount Sinai. In an atmosphere of reverence and worship, Moses ascended the mountain, where God descended in fire, smoke, and thunder. The mountain itself became a meeting place between heaven and earth, signifying the power of worship to create sacred access points to God's glory.

On Mount Sinai, Moses received the Ten Commandments and profound revelations about God's character and covenant. Each time Moses entered God's presence, he emerged transformed, his face radiating with the glory of God (Exod. 34:29–35). This physical manifestation of glory was a direct result of Moses' intimate worship and communion with almighty God.

Mount Sinai represents the transformative power of worship to open portals where divine instructions, revelations, and impartations are given. Moses' willingness to ascend into God's presence and his reverence for the holiness of the encounter demonstrate that worship positions us to receive heaven's blueprint for our lives.

Also, as we saw previously, as Paul and Silas prayed and sang hymns to God, a heavenly portal was opened, and a great earthquake shook the prison, opening all the doors and breaking the chains of the prisoners (Acts 16:26). This miraculous event was the direct result of worship, demonstrating how powerful worship is in opening heavenly portals and releasing God's power.

These biblical examples highlight the role of worship as a weapon in spiritual warfare. Worship invites God's presence into our situations, and wherever His presence comes, it pushes back the forces of darkness! When we engage in worship, we not only proclaim the truth of His sovereign power, but we also remind ourselves of His goodness, which will always disrupt the plans of the enemy. In the case of Jehoshaphat, worship turned the tide of battle without the need for physical combat. In the case of Paul and Silas, worship brought freedom and deliverance for everyone, even all the prisoners in the jail! These stories remind us that worship is a powerful tool in the hands of believers, capable of opening heavenly portals that usher in divine intervention and victory.

The Role of Music and Praise in Worship

Music has always been a central element of worship, and it plays a significant role in opening heavenly portals. The Bible is filled with references to music and praise as expressions of worship that invite God's presence.

"But now bring me a musician." Then it happened, when the musician played, that the hand of the LORD came upon him.

—2 KINGS 3:15, NKJV

This passage occurs in the context of the prophet Elisha seeking guidance from God during a time of crisis. The kings of Israel, Judah, and Edom approached him for prophetic direction as they faced the threat of war and a dire lack of water for their armies. Initially, Elisha expressed reluctance due to his disdain for King Jehoram of Israel. However, out of respect for King Jehoshaphat of Judah, he agreed to inquire of the Lord.

Elisha's request for a musician before seeking the word of the Lord is deeply significant. It reveals that music is not just a means of artistic expression but a spiritual tool that can prepare the atmosphere for divine revelation. When the musician played, the "hand of the LORD" came upon Elisha, and he received a prophetic word.

The story of David playing the harp for King Saul is another powerful example of how music can usher us into God's presence and bring spiritual relief. When Saul was tormented by an evil spirit, David would play the harp, and the Bible records, "Whenever the spirit from God came on Saul, David would take up his lyre and play. Then relief would come to Saul; he would feel better, and the evil spirit would leave him" (1 Sam. 16:23). David's music opened a heavenly portal that brought peace and drove away the evil spirit.

Music and praise are not just emotional expressions; they are spiritual weapons that can shift the atmosphere and open doors for God's presence to manifest. The power of music to connect the spiritual and physical realms is evident throughout Scripture. For example, as we just saw in 2 Kings 3:15–17, the prophet Elisha called for a musician when he was asked to provide prophetic insight. As the musician played, the hand of the Lord came upon Elisha, and he received a word from God. This passage illustrates that music can create an environment conducive to hearing from God, opening heavenly portals for divine communication.

In the Book of Psalms, we see numerous exhortations to praise God through music. We can do so in a variety of ways. The Bible describes various instruments we can use, or we can simply sing and dance to praise the Lord. Psalm 150:3–6 says, "Praise him with the sounding of the trumpet, praise him with the harp and lyre, praise him with timbrel and dancing, praise him with the strings and pipe, praise him with the clash of cymbals, praise him with resounding cymbals. Let everything that has breath praise the LORD." Engaging in musical worship with a sincere heart opens heavenly portals, allowing God's power to flow and bringing transformation to the worshipper and their environment. Whether through a simple melody sung in solitude or a full band leading a congregation, music has the power to usher in God's presence and facilitate encounters with the divine.

The Power of Sound and Frequency

Sound is a divine signature. It is one of the oldest languages of both heaven and earth. Before form, before function, before flesh— there was frequency.

Genesis 1:3 declares, "Then God said, 'Let there be light'; and there was light" (NKJV). Light, which travels in waves, was preceded by sound: God's voice. In the beginning, vibration initiated creation. God did not build the cosmos with His hands; He spoke it into existence. The universe, therefore, is not merely material—it is acoustic. Everything created was formed through frequency.

> By faith we understand that the worlds were framed by the word of God, so that the things which are seen were not made of things which are visible.
> —HEBREWS 11:3, NKJV

Scientific research in quantum physics confirms what Scripture has long declared: Matter responds to frequency. Atoms, the building blocks of all physical reality, are not static. They vibrate. Even at the subatomic level, particles behave more like energy patterns than solid matter. Sound waves have the power to influence the arrangement of molecules, a principle demonstrated in cymatics—the study of visible sound vibration. When specific frequencies pass through a medium such as sand or water, they create precise geometric patterns. This is visual proof that sound can produce ordered patterns—offering a visual parallel to the biblical theme of creation through speech.

What science is now discovering, Scripture has always known: The spiritual realm is acoustic before it is visual. Psalm 33:9 states, "For He spoke, and it was done; He commanded, and it stood fast" (NKJV). His voice—His frequency—formed worlds. And because we are made in His image (Gen. 1:27), our voices carry spiritual frequency and power as well.

Biologically, the human body is designed to respond to sound. Some researchers suggest that cells may vibrate or resonate at specific frequencies. The heart responds to rhythm. Brain waves shift based on sound exposure. Studies have shown that praise music and worshipful environments can activate the parasympathetic nervous system, placing the body into a state of peace that fosters healing and restoration. This scientific principle mirrors what occurred with King Saul. When he was tormented by an evil spirit, relief came when David played the harp (1 Sam. 16:23). Worship didn't just soothe Saul; it may have affected both his inner state and spiritual atmosphere.

But not all sound opens heaven. It is sanctified sound that becomes a portal. Elisha did not request a word from the Lord until a musician—or, more specifically, a prophetic minstrel—was summoned (2 Kings 3:15). Why? Because music has the power to tune the soul to the frequency of the Spirit. Worship becomes sacred technology, calibrating the atmosphere to hear from heaven. In that moment, sound becomes a bridge between realms.

The spirit behind the sound matters. The enemy understands this, which is why music is often used to open dark portals. But when sound is consecrated—when it is offered in pure worship—it becomes an instrument of divine access.

Revelation 4:1 underscores this truth. John wrote: "And the first voice which I heard was like a trumpet speaking with me, saying, 'Come up here, and I will show you things'" (NKJV). What opened the door to the heavenly realm wasn't a visual key but a voice—a trumpetlike frequency that called John upward into another dimension.

In a world obsessed with image and entertainment, God reminds us that heaven responds to sound. Some sounds are merely noise, but the sound of a Spirit-born, faith-filled frequency can bring heavenly change into the earth. Worship brings a divine alignment. It tunes us to the frequency of the throne of grace. It heals the body, renews the mind, and strengthens the spirit. Worship is where the seen and unseen intersect.

When we truly understand the power of sound and frequency, we will no longer treat worship as a warm-up to the sermon. We will recognize it as spiritual architecture, as a portal, as the very vibration of heaven touching earth.

Creating a Lifestyle of Worship

To open heavenly portals through worship consistently, it is essential to cultivate a lifestyle of worship that goes beyond the confines of a church service or specific moments of praise. A lifestyle of worship involves living every moment in a way that honors God and reflects His glory. We must be aware of all we do, as well as the attitude in which we act, and let our actions and thoughts be worship to our God in addition to our time spent in intentional worship.

Romans 12:1 urges believers to offer their bodies as living sacrifices, holy and pleasing to God—this is their true and proper worship. This verse highlights the idea that worship is more than an activity we engage in at church. It is a way of life. When we live with a continual awareness of God's presence and a desire to please Him, we create an atmosphere where heavenly portals are constantly open.

One practical way to create a lifestyle of worship is to incorporate worship into daily routines. This can be done by setting aside time each day to worship God. You could play worship music in your home or your car, singing praises throughout the day. You can also express your gratitude to God whenever you see Him working in your life. These are simple yet powerful ways to keep heavenly portals open. In Deuteronomy 6:6–7, God instructed the Israelites to keep His commands on their hearts, to talk about them when they sat at home and when they walked along the road, when they lay down and when they got up. This continual focus on God's Word and presence is a form of worship that invites God's presence into every aspect of life.

Another key aspect of a lifestyle of worship is obedience to God's Word. Jesus said in John 14:15, "If you love me, keep my commands." Obedience is a form of worship that pleases God and invites His presence into our lives. When we walk in obedience to His Word, we align ourselves with His will, opening heavenly portals for His blessings to flow. Obedience to God's commands demonstrates a heart of worship that goes beyond lip service, showing that we honor God with our entire lives.

A lifestyle of worship is also marked by a continual response to God's revelation. When God reveals Himself—whether through Scripture, creation, a prophetic word, or a personal encounter—our response should be one of worship. This response is not limited to verbal praise. We can express our love and worship of God through our obedience, especially our acts of service to other people. In Revelation 4:11, the elders in heaven declare, "You are worthy, our Lord and God, to receive glory and honor and power, for you created all things, and by your will they were created and have their being." Their worship is a direct response to the revelation of God's majesty and creative power.

This kind of worship keeps us attuned to the presence of God and allows His blessings to flow into our lives. As we respond to God's revelations with worship, we create a cycle of divine encounter and revelation, where each act of worship leads to deeper understanding and greater experiences of God's presence.

Did you know that worship has the power to transform more than just your own life and circumstances? It can also change the environment around you. When heavenly portals are opened through worship, God's presence ushers in healing, deliverance, and restoration—whatever you may need. The Bible highlights worship as a powerful tool for spiritual warfare. It can break down strongholds and defeat the enemy.

One example of the transformative power of worship is found in the story of Jericho. God instructed Joshua and the Israelites to march around the city of Jericho for seven days, with priests carrying the ark of the covenant and blowing trumpets. On the seventh day, they were to shout with a loud voice. The Bible records that when they obeyed God's command and shouted, the walls of Jericho fell, and the city was delivered into their hands (Josh. 6:20). Worship played a central role in this victory, as it released God's power to bring down the walls.

Worship is also a catalyst for spiritual breakthroughs. When believers engage in worship, they align themselves with God's will and position themselves to receive His blessings. The story of Jericho illustrates that worship can be the key to overcoming obstacles and entering into the promises of God. The act of marching and shouting was a physical action, to be sure. But it also was a prophetic declaration of faith that activated God's power. Similarly, when we worship in the face of challenges, we are declaring our trust in God's ability to bring victory, and this faith-filled worship opens heavenly portals that allow God's intervention.

Another powerful example of worship leading to transformation is the account of King Solomon's dedication of the temple in 2 Chronicles 5:13–14. As the priests and Levites praised God with music and singing, the glory of the Lord filled the temple, so much so that the priests could not continue their service. This overwhelming manifestation of God's presence was a direct result of the collective worship of the people. It shows that worship can bring a tangible manifestation of God's glory, transforming not only the worshippers but also the physical space where worship takes place.

Worship can bring personal transformation into our lives, for when we worship God, we are changed in His presence. As we behold His glory, we are transformed into His image, from glory to glory (2 Cor. 3:18). This transformation is a result of spending time in God's presence through worship, allowing His Spirit to work in us and conform us to His likeness.

This transformation is more than a spiritual change. Our very souls are touched, and our emotions and thoughts start to change. Worship has the power to renew the mind. If you are anxious, it can bring peace to your thoughts, and sadness can dissipate into the joy of the Lord as you spend time in His presence. The act of focusing on God and His greatness shifts our perspective, helping us see our circumstances through the lens of faith rather than fear. As we continually worship, we become more like Christ, reflecting His character and embodying His nature in every area of our lives.

Philippians 4:8 emphasizes the importance of renewing the mind as part of the Christian journey: "Finally, brothers and sisters, whatever is true, whatever is noble, whatever is right, whatever is pure, whatever is lovely, whatever is admirable—if anything is excellent or praiseworthy—think about such things."

Worship plays a crucial role in this renewal process. As we worship, our minds are realigned with the truth of God's Word, and our thoughts are purified and brought into agreement with God's will. This mental renewal is essential for spiritual growth and for maintaining an open heavenly portal through which God's wisdom and guidance can flow.

In light of the powerful impact that worship has in opening heavenly portals and transforming lives, believers are encouraged to engage in worship regularly and wholeheartedly. Don't approach worship as an obligation or a duty. It is a privilege and a joy to spend time praising the King of the universe! It is an opportunity to draw near to God, to experience His love and power, and to see His kingdom come in our lives and in the world around us.

Corporate worship—gathering with other believers to worship God—is particularly powerful. When the body of Christ comes together in unity to worship, the collective faith and spiritual hunger create an environment where heavenly portals are opened, allowing God's glory to be manifested in extraordinary ways. Psalm 133:1–3 speaks of the blessing of unity among God's people: "How good and pleasant it is when God's people live together in unity!...For there the LORD bestows his blessing, even life forevermore." This blessing is often experienced in corporate worship settings, where the unity of believers invites a greater measure of God's presence.

While corporate worship is important, personal worship is equally vital. Engaging in worship on a personal level keeps the believer's heart attuned to God and helps maintain an open channel for divine communication. You can do this by singing, by praying in the Spirit, or even by dancing in the Spirit, whatever expresses your true heart to your Savior. Personal worship is the foundation that supports and enriches corporate worship, creating a continuous flow of God's presence in the believer's life.

Making worship a daily discipline involves intentionally dedicating time to focus on God, regardless of circumstances. This could involve beginning the day with worship music, taking a moment during a busy day to thank God for His blessings, or ending the day in contemplative reflection on His goodness. By integrating worship into daily routines, we ensure that our lives are continually aligned with God's will and heavenly portals remain open.

Worship is also a pathway to deeper intimacy with God. As we draw near to Him in worship, He draws near to us, as promised in

James 4:8: "Come near to God and he will come near to you." This closeness with God brings a deeper understanding of His character and His heart for His people. Worship not only invites God's presence into our lives, but it also opens our hearts to receive His love and guidance. Through worship, we cultivate a relationship with God that transcends mere knowledge, leading to a personal and experiential understanding of who He is.

Worship is a gateway to the divine, a powerful spiritual practice that opens heavenly portals and invites God's presence into our lives. Whether through music and praise or by a lifestyle of devotion, worship creates an environment where God's glory can be manifested, bringing us the victory God has ready and waiting for us. As we engage in worship—both corporately and personally—we tap into the limitless resources of heaven and experience the fullness of God's love and power.

Let worship be more than just an event or a routine in your life. Let it become the heartbeat of your relationship with your God! As you make worship a central part of your daily walk with God, you will see the heavens open over your life, and God's divine presence will flow into every area, bringing His kingdom on earth as it is in heaven.

Activation Prayer

Heavenly Father, I come before You with a heart full of gratitude and awe for the gift of worship. Thank You for inviting me into Your presence and for opening heavenly portals that allow me to experience Your transformative power.

Lord, I ask that You teach me to worship in spirit and in truth, with a heart that is fully surrendered to You. Let my worship not be confined to moments or songs but become the very essence of my daily life. May I live as a living sacrifice, holy and pleasing to You, and may my every word, thought, and action reflect Your glory.

Father, as I worship, I invite Your kingdom to come and Your will to be done on earth as it is in heaven. I ask that You open the heavens in every area of my life. Let Your presence flow, bringing transformation in my world.

Lord, may my worship silence the noise of fear and doubt, and may it amplify the truth of Your power, love, and faithfulness. Empower me to use worship as a weapon in spiritual warfare, declaring Your sovereignty over every challenge I face.

I thank You for every encounter and every revelation of Your glory. May my worship continually create an atmosphere where heaven meets earth, and may I always carry the weight of Your presence with humility and reverence. In Jesus' mighty name, amen.

DID YOU KNOW?

Group singing, such as in worship, increases the production of oxytocin—a hormone linked to bonding and trust—while synchronizing heart rates among participants. This physiological unity reflects the spiritual power of corporate worship to align believers and invite God's presence.

PORTALS IN POP CULTURE:
The Mandela Effect

Coined in 2009, the Mandela Effect describes collective false memories, such as the belief that Nelson Mandela died in the 1980s. Some theorists attribute this phenomenon to shifts caused by interdimensional portals altering reality.

CHAPTER 6

THE WORD OF GOD AS A PORTAL OPENER

I VIVIDLY REMEMBER A season I call the "dark night of the soul." I had just experienced a series of severe betrayals and losses in my personal life, in my ministry, and in every area that mattered to me. I felt like everything I had worked for was crumbling around me. The weight of confusion and discouragement bore heavily on me, leaving me completely drained. I cried out to the Lord because no one around me could truly understand or empathize with the depths of my pain.

In that moment of brokenness, the Lord directed me to open my Bible to Psalm 27. As I began reading, the words leaped off the page and into my spirit: "The LORD is my light and my salvation—whom shall I fear? The LORD is the stronghold of my life—of whom shall I be afraid?" (v. 1). These words brought me both comfort and life itself. They illuminated my heart and mind, pushing away the oppressive cloud of darkness that had been hovering over me. It was as though the Word of God had infused me with divine strength and hope, empowering me to rise above my circumstances.

From that moment, everything began to shift. The Word of God gave me the courage and assurance to trust Him, even in the midst of turmoil. Shortly after that encounter, God began to show His faithfulness in miraculous ways. Destiny helpers were sent to support the ministry, and financial provision came through unexpected sources. New people were added to our church family. My family recovered in strength and courage in miraculous ways. What had been a period of profound darkness transformed into a season of restoration and testimony! The Word of the Lord had truly come to pass in my life, proving that He is my light and salvation.

The Word of God is one of the most powerful tools available to believers to open heavenly portals that bring the blessings of God into our lives. It is more than just a collection of ancient writings, as many people believe. No, it is a living, active force that carries the very breath of God. When we engage with the Word, we unlock the potential to access God's wisdom and power. This chapter explores how the Word of God serves as a portal opener, drawing on biblical examples and providing practical guidance for incorporating Scripture into daily life to experience its transformative power.

The Living Power of God's Word

We can read many books written by many anointed authors that give us insights into the problems we face in life. But not one of them can compare to the living Word of God. The Bible is not like any other book you will ever read. It is infused with the Spirit of the Lord and His authority! Hebrews 4:12 describes the dynamic nature of Scripture: "For the word of God is alive and active. Sharper than any double-edged sword, it penetrates even to dividing soul and spirit, joints and marrow; it judges the thoughts and attitudes of the heart." The Word of God is not static, and it is not passive. It will change you if you let it! It is alive and constantly at work on our hearts as we read it and meditate on its truths.

When we read and meditate on the Word of God and then (importantly) speak it forth into our lives, we can open heavenly portals. And that is when God's presence and power will begin to flow. The Word has the ability to transform us. It will break strongholds that need breaking and reveal the will of God for our lives. It is a conduit through which the divine touches the earthly realm, bringing the realities of heaven into our lives.

One of the most profound examples of the Word of God as a portal opener is found in the ministry of Jesus. In Matthew 4, Jesus was led by the Spirit into the wilderness to be tempted by the devil. Each time the devil tempted Him, Jesus responded with the Word of God, saying, "It is written…" (Matt. 4:4, 7, 10). By declaring Scripture, Jesus opened a heavenly portal that empowered Him to resist the devil and overcome the temptation. This account illustrates the power of the Word to open portals of strength and victory in the face of spiritual challenges.

The Word of God also brings us spiritual vitality as we give it a place of priority in our lives. Jesus emphasized the importance of living by every word that comes from the mouth of God, saying, "Man shall not live on bread alone, but on every word that comes from the mouth of God" (Matt. 4:4). Just as physical food sustains the body, the Word of God sustains the spirit. Engaging with Scripture daily feeds the soul, providing spiritual nourishment that strengthens faith and keeps us connected to God's life-giving power. This daily engagement with the Word opens heavenly portals that allow God's goodness to flow into every area of life.

The Word of God serves as a light and guide, directing believers on the path of righteousness and opening portals of divine revelation and understanding. Psalm 119:105 declares, "Your word is a lamp for my feet, a light on my path." This imagery of light emphasizes the role of Scripture in illuminating the way for us. It dispels darkness and gives us clarity whenever we are confused or uncertain about which way to go or what decision to make. The lamp is for our present state, while the light is for direction concerning the future.

When we engage with the Word of God, we invite divine guidance into our lives, opening portals of wisdom and insight. The Bible is filled with practical principles and promises that apply to every aspect of life. If you have a decision to make, seek God's will through His Word. If you are facing a challenge, find strength in the promises of the Word. If you are seeking direction, turn to the Word. It opens a portal to God's perspective and His perfect will.

The story of Joshua serves as a powerful example of how the Word of God acts as both a guide and a portal opener. After the death of Moses, Joshua was tasked with leading the Israelites into the Promised Land. God gave Joshua a specific instruction regarding the importance of the Word: "Keep this Book of the Law always on your lips; meditate on it day and night, so that you may be careful to do everything written in it. Then you will be prosperous and successful" (Josh. 1:8). By consistently meditating on and obeying the Word, Joshua opened a portal to God's favor and success in his leadership. As a result, the Israelites witnessed the fulfillment of God's promises, entering the land that had been promised to them.

The Word of God provides us with divine revelation. Through Scripture, God reveals His character, His plans, and His purposes. This revelation is essential for understanding God's will and aligning our lives with His kingdom. In Proverbs 29:18, the Bible states, "Where there is no revelation, people cast off restraint; but blessed is the one who heeds wisdom's instruction." Engaging with the Word opens a portal to divine revelation, enabling believers to live with purpose and direction. This revelation often comes as the Holy Spirit illuminates Scripture. You can receive fresh insight and understanding of the Bible that will apply directly to your life and circumstances if you ask the Holy Spirit for His help as you read.

The Transformative Power of Meditating on the Word

Meditating on the Word of God is a key practice that can transform the believer's life. Biblical meditation involves focusing the mind and heart on Scripture. When you read a verse, spend some time pondering its meaning and allowing it to penetrate deeply into your soul. Unlike the emptying of the mind found in some forms of meditation, biblical meditation is about filling the mind with God's truth. It is a form of silent prayer, where one can connect to the Holy Spirit by engaging the mind.

In Psalm 1:1–3, the psalmist described the blessedness of the person who meditates on the Word: "Blessed is the one who does not walk in step with the wicked or stand in the way that sinners take or sit in the company of mockers, but whose delight is in the law of the LORD, and who meditates on his law day and night. That person is like a tree planted by streams of water, which yields its fruit in season and whose leaf does not wither—whatever they do prospers." This passage highlights the transformative power of meditating on the Word, which opens a continual portal of God's blessings in our lives.

Meditating on the Word allows it to take root in your heart. Soon it will influence your thoughts and attitudes and therefore your actions. It enables you to internalize God's truth, making it a guiding force in your daily life. This process of internalization opens a portal to God's wisdom and strength, providing the spiritual resources you need to navigate life's challenges.

Meditating on Scripture is a powerful way to foster spiritual growth and maturity. As believers meditate on the Word, they allow it to shape their worldview. The more time you spend in the Bible, the more your own desires will align with God's and your mind will be renewed. This process of transformation is described in John 17:17, "Sanctify them by Your truth. Your word is truth" (NKJV). Through meditation, your mind is renewed, and lasting change and spiritual growth are the result. As the Word becomes deeply rooted in your heart, it produces fruit in your life, leading to increased wisdom and Christlikeness.

Speaking and Declaring the Word

The spoken word carries immense power, and when believers declare the Word of God, they open heavenly portals that release divine authority and intervention. Proverbs 18:21 states, "The tongue has the power of life and death, and those who love it will eat its fruit." This verse underscores the significance of the words we speak and the potential they have to shape our reality.

Speaking and declaring Scripture is a powerful way to activate the promises of God and to align our lives with His will. When we speak the Word in faith, it becomes a portal opener, inviting God's presence and power into the situation. This practice is particularly effective in spiritual warfare, where the believer uses the Word as a weapon to combat the lies and attacks of the enemy.

An example of the power of speaking the Word is found in the ministry of Jesus when He healed the centurion's servant. The centurion demonstrated great faith by telling Jesus, "But just say the word, and my servant will be healed" (Matt. 8:8). Jesus was amazed by the centurion's faith and spoke the word of healing, which immediately opened a heavenly portal, resulting in the servant's restoration to health. This account highlights the authority of God's Word and the importance of speaking it in faith.

The creative power of the spoken word is evident from the very beginning of Scripture. In Genesis 1, God spoke the world into existence: "And God said, 'Let there be light,' and there was light" (v. 3). This creative act demonstrates the power of God's Word to bring life and order out of chaos. Further in the New Testament, we can read the writer of Hebrews bearing witness to this reality when he penned these words in Hebrews 11:3: "By faith we understand that the worlds were framed by the word of God, so that the things which are seen were not made of things which are visible" (NKJV). As bearers of God's image, believers are called to speak words that align with His truth and creative power. When we declare God's Word over our lives, we are participating in this divine creative process, opening portals for God's will to be manifested on earth as it is in heaven.

Believers can integrate the practice of speaking and declaring the Word into their daily lives by memorizing Scripture and using it when they pray or worship God. You can speak back God's Word to Him as you remind Him of His promises, and you can share it with others in everyday conversations. By declaring God's promises and truths, you can open heavenly portals that bring the outpouring of heaven into your life. This practice not only aligns your words with God's will, but it will reinforce your faith and create an environment where God's power can be released.

One practical way to engage in speaking the Word is to create declarations based on Scripture. For example, if you are seeking peace, you might declare, "I cast all my anxiety on Him because He cares for me." (See 1 Peter 5:7.) If you need strength, you might declare, "I can do all this through Him who gives me strength." (See Philippians 4:13.) Speaking these truths aloud invites God's presence into the situation and opens portals for His promises to manifest.

The Word as a Weapon in Spiritual Warfare

The Word of God is described as a sword in the spiritual arsenal of the believer. In Ephesians 6:17, Paul referred to it as "the sword of the Spirit, which is the word of God." This imagery emphasizes the role of Scripture as a weapon in spiritual warfare, capable of cutting through the lies and attacks of the enemy.

In spiritual battles, the Word of God is indispensable. It is through the Word that we can stand firm against the enemy's schemes and resist temptation. Just as Jesus used the Word to over-come Satan's temptations in the wilderness, we can use the Word today to open portals of victory and protection in our lives.

The Word of God functions both defensively and offensively in spiritual warfare. Defensively, it protects the believer's mind and heart from the enemy's attacks. When confronted with tempta-tion, accusations, or fear, believers can rely on the truth of God's Word to shield them from lies and discouragement. Offensively, the Word is a powerful tool to counteract the enemy's strategies. By declaring God's promises and commands, we can push back against the forces of darkness, reclaiming ground that the enemy seeks to take.

One practical way to use the Word as a weapon is to identify specific scriptures that address the particular challenges or attacks being faced. These scriptures can be declared in prayer or meditated upon to strengthen faith and resolve. For example, when facing fear, a believer might declare the words of Psalm 27:1: "The LORD is my light and my salvation—whom shall I fear? The LORD is the stronghold of my life—of whom shall I be afraid?" By wielding the Word in this way, the believer opens a heavenly portal that brings God's strength and courage into the situation.

Another effective method for incorporating the Word into daily life is through Scripture memorization. By committing key verses to memory, believers can have the Word readily available in their hearts and minds, even in situations where they do not have access to a Bible. Memorized Scripture can be recalled in moments of need, opening portals of divine wisdom, comfort, and guidance. Psalm 119:11 emphasizes the importance of internalizing Scripture: "I have hidden your word in my heart that I might not sin against you." Having the Word hidden in the heart acts as a safeguard against temptation and a source of strength in times of trial.

Meditating on Scripture throughout the day is another powerful practice that involves reflecting on a verse or passage, allowing its meaning to sink deeply into the heart and the mind. Meditation on the Word can even affect the physical body. As we meditate on the Word, we allow it to influence our thoughts and behaviors, creating a continuous flow of God's truth and power in our lives.

Integrating the Word into daily routines can also help believers stay connected to God's guidance and presence. You could start your day with a Scripture reading, using the verses you read as prayer prompts. Or you could spend some time reflecting on a passage during a quiet moment in the day. Journaling about what God is revealing through His Word can also help us internalize Scripture and apply it to daily life. By making the Word a regular part of your routine, you can keep heavenly portals open, allowing God's wisdom and guidance to flow into every area of your life.

Another approach is to use Scripture in conversations and inter-actions with others. Sharing a verse of encouragement, offering a prayer based on Scripture, or discussing a biblical principle in a group setting can reinforce the truths of God's Word in the believer's life and the lives of those around them.

Finally, we are encouraged to live out the Word in our daily actions and decisions. James 1:22–25 calls believers to be doers of the Word, not just hearers: "Do not merely listen to the word, and so deceive yourselves. Do what it says. Anyone who listens to the word but does not do what it says is like someone who looks at his face in a mirror and, after looking at himself, goes away and immediately forgets what he looks like. But whoever looks intently into the perfect law that gives freedom, and continues in it—not forgetting what they have heard, but doing it—they will be blessed in what they do."

Living out the Word means making decisions that align with Scripture, treating others with the love and respect that Jesus taught, and being a witness to the transformative power of God's Word in action. As you intentionally practice these things each day, your faith will consistently be strengthened. People around you will start to notice, and your life will become a testimony to others, by God's grace.

The Word of God is a powerful portal opener, capable of bringing divine wisdom, guidance, protection, and transformation into the lives of believers. When you actively engage with Scripture, you allow God's presence and power to flow freely in your life.

As you continue to incorporate the Word into your daily life, remember that you are not just reading words on a page, but you are engaging with the living, active Word of God. It holds the power to transform your life! Let the Word be your guide and your source of strength. Use it as your greatest weapon in spiritual warfare. As you do, you will see the realities of heaven manifested on earth and God's will accomplished in and through your life.

Activation Prayer

Heavenly Father, I thank You for the gift of Your Word, which is alive, powerful, and active in our lives. Thank You for the light it brings to my darkest moments, the guidance it offers when I am lost, and the strength it provides when I am weary. Your Word is a lamp to my feet and a light to my path, and I am grateful for its transformative power.

Lord, I ask that You help me engage with Your Word daily. I commit to meditate on its truth and hide it in my heart. May Your Word become a portal through which Your wisdom and peace flow into every area of my life. Teach me to speak and declare Your promises with faith, knowing that Your Word never returns void.

Father, I pray for those who may be struggling to hear from You or who are in a season of confusion and despair. Let the truth of Your Word pierce through the darkness and bring clarity and hope. May Your Word continue to guide us and empower us all as we walk in obedience to Your will.

Thank You, Lord, for the assurance that Your Word is unchanging and full of life. I commit myself to living by every word that comes from Your mouth, trusting that it will lead me into victory and draw me closer to You. In Jesus' matchless name, I pray. Amen.

DID YOU KNOW?

Reading and meditating on Scripture activates neural circuits associated with moral reasoning and empathy. This rewiring of the brain reflects how God's Word transforms believers, opening spiritual portals to wisdom and guidance.

PORTALS IN POP CULTURE:
The Bermuda Triangle

For decades, reports of planes and ships disappearing in this region of the Atlantic Ocean have sparked speculation about portals to other dimensions. Theories range from natural phenomena to supernatural gateways. Though these theories are fascinating, they remind us how easily curiosity can drift into distraction. As believers, our focus must remain fixed on Christ. He is the true gate, the only way, and our anchor in both the seen and unseen realms.

CHAPTER 7

THE ROLE OF FAITH IN ENGAGING PORTALS

TRUST YOU'VE BEEN enjoying our journey so far. Let's go deeper! Faith is the key that unlocks the doors of the spiritual realm, enabling believers to engage with heavenly portals and access the divine resources that God has made available. Without faith, it is impossible to please God or to fully experience the power and presence that flows through these spiritual gateways. This chapter delves into the crucial role of *faith* in engaging portals and obtaining the blessings of the Lord.

I remember ministering in New York during a powerful service where the presence of God was tangible. As I began to minister the Word of the Lord and prophesy over individuals, there was one particular person whom God highlighted for a unique prophetic act. The Lord gave me specific instructions that seemed unusual at the time, but I sensed they were crucial for what He wanted to accomplish.

I had my prayer shawl with me, and I felt let by the Spirit to use it in a prophetic gesture. I asked my assistant to bring it to me. Laying the prayer shawl on the ground, I explained to the individual that they were about to enact a prophetic act of faith. I instructed them to take a few steps backward, symbolizing the challenges and setbacks they had been facing in life. Then I told them to run forward and step over the threshold created by the prayer shawl, representing a crossing into a new season of restoration.

At first, the gesture might have seemed strange, even foolish, but faith often requires stepping beyond the natural and into the supernatural (1 Cor. 2:14). This individual, full of faith and expectation, obeyed without hesitation. As they ran forward and crossed over the threshold, there was a spiritual eruption in the atmosphere. It felt as though heaven had opened, and a wave of Holy Spirit power swept through the room. The entire congregation erupted into celebration, praising and worshipping the Lord Jesus with fervor.

Not long after, we received a powerful testimony from this person. They shared how that prophetic act of faith had catalyzed a series of miracles in their life. Financial provision came unexpectedly. Longstanding family issues were resolved, and most importantly, their children came to know the Lord. Additionally, they experienced healing in their body that they had been praying for. This testimony served as a profound reminder that faith is not passive—it requires action, even in the face of uncertainty. When faith and prophetic obedience align, heavenly portals open, and the miraculous is released.

The Foundation of Faith in Engaging Portals

Faith is the foundational principle upon which our relationship with God is built. Hebrews 11:1 defines *faith* as "the substance of things hoped for, the evidence of things not seen" (NKJV). This means that faith involves believing in the reality of things that cannot be perceived with the natural senses but are nonetheless true according to God's Word. When it comes to engaging heavenly portals, faith is the currency that activates and opens these gateways, allowing God's presence and His grace to flow into our lives.

The Bible is replete with examples of how faith opens portals to the divine. One of the most well-known instances is the story of the centurion in Matthew 8:5–13. The centurion approached Jesus, asking Him to heal his servant who was paralyzed and suffering terribly. Jesus offered to come to the centurion's home, but the centurion replied, "Lord, I do not deserve to have you come under my roof. But just say the word, and my servant will be healed" (v. 8). Jesus marveled at the centurion's faith and declared, "Truly I tell you, I have not found anyone in Israel with such great faith" (v. 10). The servant was healed that very moment, demonstrating how faith opens a portal for God's miraculous power to be released.

Many people think faith involves some type of intellectual assent, and they try to work themselves up mentally to "believe." That's not what faith is! It is really a deep-seated trust in God and His promises. It is the assurance that what God has spoken is true, regardless of circumstances or visible evidence. This kind of faith is essential for engaging with heavenly portals, as it aligns the believer's heart and mind with the reality of God's kingdom.

Faith serves as a bridge between the natural world and the supernatural realm, enabling us to access the unseen realities of God's kingdom and bring them into manifestation in the physical world. It brings the invisible into the visible (Heb. 11:3). By exercising faith, we open portals for the supernatural power of God to intervene in their natural circumstances. And miracles are often the result!

Throughout Scripture, we find numerous examples of individuals who engaged with heavenly portals through faith, resulting in divine intervention and miraculous outcomes. These stories serve as powerful reminders of the importance of faith in our own spiritual journeys.

- **Abraham's faith and the portal of promise:**
  Abraham is often referred to as the father of faith, and his life exemplifies how faith opens portals to God's promises. In Genesis 12, God called Abraham to leave his homeland and go to a land that He would show him. Despite not knowing where he was going, Abraham obeyed, trusting in God's promise. His faith opened a portal to a covenant relationship with God, leading to the fulfillment of the promise that his descendants would become a great nation (vv. 1–4). Abraham's journey was marked by numerous instances when his faith activated heavenly portals, leading to divine encounters, such as the appearance of God in Genesis 18 to reaffirm the promise of a son.

- **The woman with the issue of blood:** In Mark 5:25–34, we read the story of a woman who had been suffering from a bleeding condition for twelve years. Despite the crowd pressing around Jesus, she believed that if she could just touch His cloak, she would be healed. Her faith opened a portal to divine healing, and immediately her bleeding stopped. Jesus recognized the power that had gone out from Him and said to her, "Daughter, your faith has healed you. Go in peace and be freed from your suffering" (v. 34). This story illustrates the power of personal faith in accessing God's healing power and opening portals of restoration and wholeness.

- **The faith of the friends of the paralytic:** In Luke 5:17–26, a group of friends brought a paralyzed man to Jesus, but because of the crowd, they could not reach Him. Undeterred, they climbed onto the roof, removed the tiles, and lowered the man on his mat into the middle of the crowd, right in front of Jesus. Their faith opened a portal to divine healing and forgiveness, as Jesus not only healed the man but also forgave his sins: "When Jesus saw their faith, he said, 'Friend, your sins are forgiven'" (v. 20). This example emphasizes the collective power of faith in opening portals, showing that sometimes it is the faith of a community that brings about a miracle.

These examples illustrate that faith is not passive! All of these people had to *act* with *perseverance* in order to receive their miracles! The individuals in these stories took bold steps of faith, and as a result, they experienced the opening of heavenly portals that brought about miraculous change in their lives.

The Greek word for *faith*, *pistis* (πίστις), signifies trust or confidence, particularly in God or His promises. Its connection to the

English word *piston* (a mechanical part of an engine) is prophetic. Just as a piston operates by creating movement and energy when acted upon by external force (e.g., combustion in an engine), *pistis* (faith) generates spiritual movement and power when it responds to God's promises, driving the "engine" of a believer's life and actions. Faith, like a piston, translates potential into action.

Faith requires taking practical steps that demonstrate trust in God's promises. The woman with the issue of blood took a risk by pushing through the crowd, and the friends of the paralytic demonstrated their faith through their creative and persistent efforts to bring their friend to Jesus. These actions were outward expressions of their inner faith, and they activated the power of God in their situations. James 2:17 reinforces this principle: "In the same way, faith by itself, if it is not accompanied by action, is dead." True faith is always accompanied by actions that align with God's will, and these actions open portals for His divine intervention.

Overcoming Doubt and Unbelief

While faith is powerful, it is often challenged by doubt and unbelief. These spiritual hindrances can prevent believers from fully engaging with heavenly portals and experiencing the fullness of God's blessings. It is essential to recognize and overcome these obstacles to maintain a strong and active faith.

Doubt and unbelief are often rooted in fear. Past disappointments or a limited understanding of God's nature and promises can make it hard to believe sometimes. In Mark 9:23–24, a father brought his demon-possessed son to Jesus, asking for help. Jesus responded, "'Everything is possible for one who believes.' Immediately the boy's father exclaimed, 'I do believe; help me overcome my unbelief!'" This honest admission reflects the internal struggle that many believers face when their faith is mixed with doubt. However, the father's request for help was itself an act of faith, and Jesus responded by healing his son.

Doubt is a natural part of the human experience, especially in situations where faith is being tested. However, it is important not to allow doubt to take root and undermine faith. One way to combat doubt is to immerse oneself in the Word of God. Romans 10:17 tells us, "So then faith comes by hearing, and hearing by the word of God" (NKJV). Regular exposure to Scripture strengthens faith by reminding us of God's character. His promises and instances of His past faithfulness appear in the Bible for the purpose of helping us believe. By focusing on God's Word, believers can counteract the lies and fears that feed doubt.

Additionally, prayer is a vital tool in combating doubt. By presenting doubts and fears before God through prayer, we can receive the strength and assurance needed to remain steadfast in faith. Philippians 4:6–7 encourages us to bring everything to God in prayer: "Do not be anxious about anything, but in every situation, by prayer and petition, with thanksgiving, present your requests to God. And the peace of God, which transcends all understanding, will guard your hearts and your minds in Christ Jesus." This peace is a by-product of faith and acts as a safeguard against doubt and unbelief.

Gratitude is another powerful faith-building practice. By regularly giving thanks for God's blessings, both big and small, believers reinforce their trust in God's goodness and faithfulness. Gratitude shifts the focus from what is lacking to what God has already provided, creating an atmosphere of faith that opens portals to even greater experiences in God. Again, Philippians 4:6 advises us to present our prayers and petitions to God "with thanksgiving." Gratitude fosters a mindset of abundance rather than scarcity, encouraging us to trust God for even greater things.

Being part of a community of faith is also important. Fellow believers can provide encouragement, share testimonies, and pray for one another, helping to bolster faith in times of struggle. Hebrews 10:24–25 encourages us to "consider how we may spur one another on toward love and good deeds, not giving up meeting together, as some are in the habit of doing, but encouraging one another." This mutual support is key to maintaining strong faith and effectively engaging with heavenly portals.

Faith is not static. It is dynamic! And it must be nurtured and strengthened continually. There are several practices that believers can adopt to sustain and grow our faith, enabling us to engage consistently with heavenly portals.

Stepping out in faith

Faith is like a muscle that grows stronger with use. By taking steps of faith, even when the outcome is uncertain, believers can experience God's faithfulness firsthand. These experiences reinforce trust in God and build confidence to engage with heavenly portals.

Taking action based on faith is a crucial component of spiritual growth and engaging with the divine. Whether it's making a decision that aligns with God's Word, sharing the gospel with someone, or trusting God with a difficult situation, each step of faith strengthens our connection to God and opens portals for His intervention.

Focusing on God, not circumstances

To maintain strong faith, it is important to keep one's eyes on God rather than on the circumstances. Peter's experience of walking on water in Matthew 14:28–31 illustrates this principle. As long as Peter focused on Jesus, he was able to walk on the water. However, the moment his attention shifted to the wind and waves, he began to sink. Jesus reached out and caught him, saying, "You of little faith, why did you doubt?" (v. 31). This story serves as a reminder to keep our faith anchored in God, regardless of external circumstances. By keeping our focus on God's character and promises, we can maintain strong faith even in the face of challenges.

Faith is often tested during trials and difficult circumstances. These tests are opportunities for us to deepen our trust in God and prove the genuineness of our faith. James 1:2–4 encourages believers to "consider it pure joy, my brothers and sisters, whenever you face trials of many kinds, because you know that the testing of your faith produces perseverance. Let perseverance finish its work so that you may be mature and complete, not lacking anything." We can look at trials as obstacles to be overcome, but they are so much more than that. They are opportunities for spiritual growth. By embracing challenges with faith, believers can experience the opening of portals that bring divine strength and provide us with the endurance we need to persevere.

Living by faith is not just about mustering up "belief" during moments of crisis or need. As we practice a daily lifestyle of faith, it positions us to engage with heavenly portals and experience the fullness of God's kingdom! Hebrews 11:6 emphasizes the importance of faith: "And without faith it is impossible to please God, because anyone who comes to him must believe that he exists and that he rewards those who earnestly seek him."

Believers are encouraged to cultivate a life of faith by trusting God in every area. What do you need today? Financial provision? Guidance in a personal relationship? Healing in your body? Living by faith creates an environment where heavenly portals are consistently open, allowing God's blessings to flow.

Living by faith as a daily commitment

Living by faith means trusting God even when the outcome is uncertain or when the circumstances seem impossible. It means believing that God's Word is true and that He is able to do what He has promised. As you step out in faith, you will see the power of God manifest in your life, opening heavenly portals. The realities of heaven will invade your earthly experience and change your life!

In practical terms, living by faith involves making decisions based on God's Word rather than on fear or doubt. It means seeking God's direction in prayer and being willing to follow His leading, even when it requires stepping out of your comfort zone. It also means speaking and declaring God's promises over your life, believing that what He has said will come to pass.

One of the greatest examples of living by faith is found in the life of Abraham. Despite his old age and the seeming impossibility of

God's promise to give him a son, Abraham "did not waver through unbelief regarding the promise of God, but was strengthened in his faith and gave glory to God, being fully persuaded that God had power to do what he had promised" (Rom. 4:20–21). Abraham's unwavering faith opened a portal to God's miraculous provision, and he became the father of many nations. His life serves as an example of how faith can bring God's promises into reality, even in the face of overwhelming odds.

Remember that faith is not a onetime event but a daily practice. By consistently turning to God, trusting in His Word, and taking steps of faith, you will grow stronger in your relationship with Him and see His hand at work in every area of your life. As you live by faith, you will become a living testimony of God's goodness, and your life will be a portal through which His kingdom comes on earth as it is in heaven.

Living by faith means developing a continual awareness of God's presence and His active role in your life. It involves recognizing that everything we do can be an opportunity to demonstrate trust in God. When faith becomes a daily practice, it transforms how you approach life's challenges and opportunities, enabling you to experience God's supernatural intervention in the ordinary moments of life.

Faith should permeate every aspect of your life, from your personal relationships and career decisions to your health and finances. When you trust God with every part of your life, you invite His guidance and favor into those areas, opening portals for His divine influence. Proverbs 3:5–6 advises, "Trust in the LORD with all your heart and lean not on your own understanding; in all your ways submit to him, and he will make your paths straight." This level of trust requires surrendering control and allowing God to lead, but it results in a life that is aligned with His will and purpose.

The journey of faith is ongoing and ever-evolving. As you continue to grow in your relationship with God, He will lead you into deeper levels of trust and dependence on Him. Each step of faith builds on the previous one, creating a solid foundation upon which you can stand when faced with new challenges. This journey is not without its trials, but each challenge is an opportunity to see God's faithfulness in a new way and experience His power in greater measure.

Practical Ways to Make Faith a Daily Practice

Making faith a part of each day is important, because each day brings its own set of new challenges. Here are some ways you can practice building your faith day by day:

Frame each day with faith. Begin your day by affirming your trust in God. This can be as simple as praying, "Lord, I trust You with today. I believe that You are guiding my steps and that Your plans for me are good." My personal favorite declaration of faith—something I've spoken every single morning for the past sixteen years and counting—is the very first thing I say upon waking, after a moment of silent meditation. Before doing anything else, I speak this aloud at least twice: "This is the day that the Lord has made; I will rejoice and be glad in it. It is a day of miracles, signs, wonders, breakthrough, and testimonies!" Starting the day with this mindset sets a foundation of faith that will carry you through whatever challenges you may face.

Face challenges with faith. When you encounter difficulties or decisions, choose to respond in faith rather than fear. Remind yourself of God's promises and His past faithfulness in your life. Declare His Word over the situation, such as, "Even though I walk through the darkest valley, I will fear no evil, for you are with me" (Ps. 23:4).

Reflect on God's faithfulness. At the end of each day, take time to reflect on how God has been faithful. Consider how He has answered prayers, provided for your needs, or given you strength to face challenges. This practice not only builds gratitude but also strengthens your faith for the future.

Share your faith. Talk about your faith with others. Share testimonies of how God has worked in your life, and encourage others to trust in Him as well. This is a powerful way to reinforce your own faith *and* help others experience God's power and presence.

Revelation 12:11 highlights the power of testimony: "They triumphed over him by the blood of the Lamb and by the word of their testimony." When believers share their experiences of God's intervention, they inspire others to trust Him in their own situations, opening portals for similar miracles to take place. Testimonies serve as powerful reminders that God is actively involved in our lives and that He is faithful to keep His promises.

The Reward of Faith

When was the last time you waited on something with *expectation*? Faith involves expecting good things from the Lord! The Bible says that God rewards those who diligently seek Him and live by faith (Heb. 11:6). The rewards of faith may come in various forms, not the least of which is answered prayer! We can also experience spiritual growth, peace in difficult times, and the greatest reward of all: eternal life with God.

The apostle Paul, under the inspiration of the Holy Spirit, beautifully wrote on this spiritual reality in Galatians 3:11: "But that no one is justified by the law in the sight of God is evident, for 'the just shall live by faith'" (NKJV). One of the greatest rewards of living by faith is the deepening of your relationship with God. As you trust Him and see His faithfulness in your life, your love for Him grows, and your understanding of His character deepens. This intimate relationship with God is the ultimate reward, far surpassing any material blessings.

Moreover, living by faith positions you to be a conduit of God's goodness to others. When you live by faith, you are living for more than just *you*. Other people benefit too! Your life of faith can inspire others to trust in God, and through your prayers and actions, you can help open heavenly portals that bring God's presence and power into their lives.

Faith is the essential ingredient for engaging with heavenly portals and experiencing the fullness of God's kingdom in your life, paving the way for you to unlock the divine resources available to you and see God's promises fulfilled. As you cultivate a life of faith, you will witness the opening of portals that brings God's amazing blessings, right where you need them the most.

Ultimately, living by faith is about maintaining an eternal perspective. While faith enables you to experience God's blessings in this life, it also keeps you focused on the ultimate reward—eternal life with God. Hebrews 11:13–16 describes the heroes of faith who lived with an eternal perspective: "All these people were still living by faith when they died. They did not receive the things promised; they only saw them and welcomed them from a distance, admitting that they were foreigners and strangers on earth....Instead, they were longing for a better country—a heavenly one. Therefore God is not ashamed to be called their God, for he has prepared a city for them."

Living with an eternal perspective means understanding that the trials and challenges of this life are temporary and that the true reward of faith is found in the life to come. This perspective helps you persevere in faith, even when the immediate outcomes are not what you expected, knowing that God's promises are ultimately fulfilled in eternity.

As you continue on your faith journey, be encouraged that you are not alone. God is with you every step of the way. He stands ready to guide you and meet your needs. He is faithful to His promises, and as you trust in Him, you will see His hand at work in your life. Keep pressing forward in faith, knowing that God is leading you into greater dimensions of His presence and purpose and into deeper intimacy with Him.

Activation Prayer

Heavenly Father, I thank You for the gift of faith, which connects me to Your promises and opens portals to Your power and presence. Lord, I ask that You strengthen my faith and help me trust You in every situation, no matter how uncertain or challenging it may seem. Increase my ability to step out in boldness and obedience, knowing that You are faithful to fulfill what You have spoken.

Father, teach me to live by faith daily, not just in moments of crisis. I want to follow You in every aspect of my life. Help me keep my eyes fixed on You, not on my circumstances, so that I may walk confidently in Your will. Remind me that faith requires action, and give me the courage to take those steps that align with Your Word and Your purposes.

Lord, I pray for those who are struggling with doubt or unbelief. Meet them in their place of need and fill their hearts with the assurance of Your love. Let Your Word come alive in their spirits, building their faith and opening divine portals for miracles and healing.

Thank You for being a God who rewards those who diligently seek You. May my life be marked by unwavering faith, and may I become a vessel through which Your kingdom comes on earth as it is in heaven. I give You all the glory, honor, and praise. In Jesus' mighty name, I pray. Amen.

DID YOU KNOW?

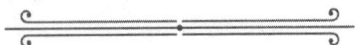

Research shows that individuals with strong levels of faith experience higher levels of resilience during adversity. This resilience is linked to the brain's release of dopamine, reinforcing hope and demonstrating how faith engages heavenly portals and strengthens believers.

PORTALS IN POP CULTURE:
NASA's Magnetic Portals to the Sun (2014)

NASA scientists have discovered magnetic connections between the earth and the sun that open and close every few minutes (flux transfer events). While scientific, these discoveries showcase striking parallels to spiritual portals that connect different dimensions.

CHAPTER 8

THE DANGERS OF ENGAGING WITH DEMONIC PORTALS

I RECALL MINISTERING TO a young man who came to the ministry seeking hope, though he seemed deeply burdened by life's hardships. As I began to minister to him, the Holy Spirit revealed layers of generational chains and curses at work in his life. Spiritually, I discerned the shadow of death looming over him, which made me ask specific questions about his life and circumstances.

He confirmed that his brother had been murdered and that many of his close friends who had engaged in destructive lifestyles had met the same fate. His life was marked by loss, grief, trauma, and a sense of abandonment. However, the Spirit made it clear that his time for freedom and deliverance had come.

As I continued ministering, I noticed his body was covered with tattoos and markings from self-harm. The Spirit urged me to ask him about specific designs, and the truth began to unfold. What the young man hadn't realized was that these tattoos were more than just art. They were tied to rituals and ceremonies associated with the occult. The places he had frequented to get these tattoos were steeped in darkness, and by engaging with them, he had unknowingly opened demonic portals that allowed spiritual oppression to take root in his life.

The young man broke down as we uncovered these connections. With the guidance of the Holy Spirit, we prayed together, renouncing every tie, breaking every chain, and closing every portal that had been opened. We declared freedom over his life, calling on the power of Jesus Christ to sever these spiritual entanglements.

In that moment, God moved powerfully. The oppression lifted, and the weight that had kept him bound for so long was broken. This man, once single, broken, depressed, and without purpose, is now married with a child. His entire family serves the Lord, and he has discovered his God-given purpose. Today, he walks boldly in his calling, a testimony to the redemptive and liberating power of God.

While heavenly portals bring God's presence, blessings, and protection into our lives, there are also dark spiritual gateways known as demonic portals that invite the forces of evil. These portals can lead to oppression, bondage, and destruction, making it crucial for believers to understand the dangers associated with them and learn how to avoid or close these portals if they have been opened. This chapter delves into the risks of engaging with demonic portals. We will discover how they are opened, as well as the steps believers can take to protect themselves.

The Consequences of Opening Demonic Portals

The consequences of opening a demonic portal can be severe and far-reaching. They affect the individual involved, as well as their family and the community at large, and the repercussions can even be passed down to future generations. These consequences often manifest in various forms of spiritual and emotional oppression that can also be displayed in physical form.

Spiritual oppression

One of the most common consequences of opening a demonic portal is spiritual oppression, which can manifest as feelings of heaviness, depression, fear, and anxiety with no natural cause. It can also present as an inability to pray, read the Bible, or engage in worship, as the individual feels disconnected from God. The enemy uses this oppression to weaken the believer's spiritual life, trapping them in a cycle of despair and defeat.

Physical ailments

In some cases, demonic portals can lead to physical ailments that have no clear medical explanation. The Bible provides examples of demonic influence causing physical afflictions, as seen in Luke 13:11–13, where Jesus healed a woman who had been crippled by a spirit for eighteen years. Once the demonic influence was removed, the woman was immediately healed. This shows that some physical issues might have spiritual roots and that addressing the spiritual cause could lead to physical healing.

Mental torment

Demonic portals can also result in mental torment, manifesting as intrusive thoughts. Nightmares and a sense of hopelessness or despair are also very common. These symptoms are often the result of demonic harassment, during which the individual is subjected to a constant barrage of negative thoughts. Fear runs rampant, and the mind seems to condemn the person of even the slightest missteps. The enemy seeks to wear down the believer's mind and emotions, creating a sense of isolation and helplessness.

Destruction of relationships and finances

Demonic portals can lead to the destruction of relationships and finances. The enemy seeks to steal, kill, and destroy (John 10:10), and this intent can manifest in broken relationships. Financial instability is not uncommon, and a sense of constant turmoil or crisis in life can follow the person around. The presence of a demonic portal can create an atmosphere of strife, confusion, and lack, disrupting the peace and order God desires for His people.

The ultimate goal of the enemy in opening demonic portals is to bring destruction and separation from God. By using these portals, the enemy gains a foothold in the lives of people, even believers, with the intent of causing as much harm as possible. Understanding the enemy's agenda helps us recognize the seriousness of engaging with or allowing demonic portals to remain open. Though the enemy's tactics are subtle and deceptive, being aware of them empowers us to stand firm in our faith and take action to close any open portals.

Recognizing the Signs of a Demonic Portal

Recognizing the signs of a demonic portal is crucial for taking steps to close it and seek deliverance. Some common indicators that a demonic portal may be open include these:

- **Persistent negative patterns:** Repeated cycles of failure, destructive behavior, or persistent problems that seem resistant to change may indicate the presence of a demonic portal, often signaling a deeper spiritual issue that needs to be addressed.

- **Unexplained oppression or torment:** Sudden or persistent feelings of oppression, fear, or torment, particularly when there is no apparent natural cause, can be a sign of a demonic influence. This may manifest as a heavy atmosphere in a home or a constant sense of dread or anxiety that lingers without explanation.

- **Unholy or sinful thoughts:** Intrusive, blasphemous, or sinful thoughts that seem to come out of nowhere may indicate that a demonic portal has been opened. These thoughts can be persistent and difficult to control, suggesting that the enemy is attempting to gain influence over the individual's mind.

- **Difficulty engaging in spiritual activities:** A sudden or prolonged inability to pray or engage with God in any way, especially through reading the Bible or worship, may suggest spiritual interference from a demonic source. The enemy seeks to disconnect believers from their spiritual lifelines, making it challenging to engage in activities that draw them closer to God.

- **Strange occurrences:** Unexplained phenomena, such as objects moving, strange noises, or the sense of an evil presence, can be signs that a demonic portal is open in a particular location. These occurrences are often accompanied by a deep sense of unease or fear.

Recognizing the signs of a demonic portal calls for spiritual discernment. The Bible encourages believers to "test the spirits to see whether they are from God" (1 John 4:1). This discernment is a gift of the Holy Spirit that allows believers to differentiate between what is of God and what is of the enemy. By staying close to God through prayer, reading the Word, and living lives of holiness, we can develop the discernment needed to recognize and address any signs of demonic influence.

Steps to Close Demonic Portals

If a demonic portal has been opened, it's essential to take immediate steps to close it and seek God's deliverance. The following steps can help believers close these portals and restore spiritual protection in their lives:

1. **Repent and renounce.** The first step in closing a demonic portal is to repent of any sins or actions that may have caused it to open. This involves confessing the sin to God, asking for His forgiveness, and renouncing any involvement in occult practices or sinful behavior. James 4:7–8 says, "Submit yourselves, then, to God. Resist the devil, and he will flee from you. Come near to God and he will come near to you." Submitting to God and resisting the enemy are key to closing the portal.

2. **Break curses and generational ties.** If the portal was opened through a curse or generational sin, it's important to break these ties in the name of Jesus. This can be achieved through prayer and declaring that the curse or generational sin is null and void through the power of Christ's sacrifice. Galatians 3:13 affirms, "Christ redeemed us from the curse of the law by becoming a curse for us," granting the authority to break any curses.

3. **Remove unholy objects or influences.** Any objects, symbols, or influences associated with the occult or idolatry should be removed from one's life and home. This may involve destroying items, removing the items from the environment, or distancing oneself from environments or relationships that encourage sinful behavior.

4. **Seek deliverance.** In some cases, seeking deliverance from a trusted minister may be necessary. Deliverance, the process of casting out demonic influences that have gained access through a portal, was a key aspect of Jesus' ministry, and He gave His followers authority over demons (Mark 16:17). Seeking deliverance can provide freedom from spiritual oppression and close the demonic portal.

5. **Fill the void with God's presence.** After closing a demonic portal, it's important to fill the void with God's presence. Ephesians 5:18–19 encourages believers to be filled with the Spirit, speaking to one another with psalms, hymns, and spiritual songs. By continually inviting the Holy Spirit into your life, you create an environment that is hostile to demonic influences and conducive to God's presence.

The Holy Spirit plays an important role in the deliverance process. Through the power of the Holy Spirit, believers can effectively close demonic portals and break free from the influence of the enemy. The Holy Spirit provides the guidance and strength needed to confront and overcome demonic forces. By relying on the Holy Spirit, each of us can experience true freedom and maintain a life that is protected from the enemy's attacks.

Protecting Yourself and Others from Demonic Portals

Prevention is the best strategy when it comes to demonic portals. By understanding how these portals are opened and taking proactive steps to avoid them, you can protect yourself and your loved ones from spiritual harm.

Stay rooted in God's Word. Regular study and meditation on the Bible keep you grounded in God's truth, enabling you to recognize and reject any influences that are not from Him. Psalm 119:11 says, "I have hidden your word in my heart that I might not sin against you." Knowing God's Word equips you to stand firm against the enemy's schemes and prevents the opening of demonic portals.

Be discerning about what you engage with. Be mindful of the media, entertainment, and activities you choose to engage in. Avoid anything that glorifies the occult or any type of sinful behavior. Philippians 4:8 encourages believers to think about things that are true, noble, right, pure, lovely, admirable, excellent, and praiseworthy. Engaging in wholesome and godly activities helps protect against exposure to demonic influences.

Pray for protection. Regularly pray for God's protection over yourself, your family, and your home. Ask God to place a hedge of protection around you and keep you safe from the enemy's attacks. Psalm 91 is a powerful passage to pray for protection, as it declares God's promises to shield and deliver those who trust in Him.

Be vigilant in your spiritual life. Stay alert to the enemy's tactics, and remain vigilant in your spiritual life. First Peter 5:8 warns, "Be alert and of sober mind. Your enemy the devil prowls around like a roaring lion looking for someone to devour." By staying spiritually awake and alert, you can detect any attempts by the enemy to open a portal in your life and take immediate action to prevent that from happening.

Teach others. If you have children or others in your care, teach them about the dangers of demonic portals and how to avoid them. Guide them in making wise choices, and encourage them to seek God's guidance in all they do. Proverbs 22:6 advises, "Start children off on the way they should go, and even when they are old they will not turn from it."

Maintaining a disciplined spiritual life is essential in protecting against demonic portals. The spiritual disciplines we've discussed throughout this book will create a strong foundation that aligns you with God's will and shields you from the enemy's influence. These disciplines also strengthen your relationship with God, making it easier to hear His voice and follow His guidance. By making spiritual discipline a regular part of your life, you can safeguard yourself and others from the dangers of demonic portals.

Demonic portals are a serious threat to the spiritual well-being of believers, but they can be avoided or closed through repentance and turning from sin, as well as reliance on God's power. Understanding how these portals are opened, as well as the consequences of engaging with them, is the first step in protecting yourself and others from their destructive influence.

By staying rooted in God's Word and living a life of holiness, you can keep demonic portals closed and maintain a strong spiritual defense. Remember, Jesus has already won the victory over the powers of darkness, and through Him, you have the authority to close any portal the enemy may try to open in your life. Invite His presence into your life daily!

As you continue to walk in faith and obedience, you will experience the fullness of God's protection and blessings, ensuring that your life remains a place where only heavenly portals are open, allowing the light and love of God to flow freely.

Activation Prayer

Heavenly Father, I thank You for the authority and power You have given me through Jesus Christ to overcome the works of the enemy. Lord, I ask for Your discernment to recognize any areas in my life where demonic portals may have been opened. I repent of any sin. I renounce the enemy and close these gateways through the power of Your name.

Fill me with Your Holy Spirit and surround me with Your protection. Guard my heart and my mind. Father, protect my home from any influence of darkness, and strengthen me to walk in holiness and truth. May my life be a dwelling place for Your presence, where only heavenly portals remain open.

Thank You, Lord, for Your victory over the powers of darkness. I trust in Your promises and stand firm in the freedom You have given me. In Jesus' mighty name, I pray. Amen.

DID YOU KNOW?

Psychologists warn that engaging in occult practices or horror content can trigger hyperarousal in the amygdala, increasing fear responses. This warning aligns with the spiritual truth that opening demonic portals invites darkness, fear, and spiritual oppression.

PORTALS IN POP CULTURE:
Supernatural (2005–2020 TV series)

This long-running show frequently dealt with portals to "hell and heaven." Specific episodes portrayed how rituals, relics, or sacrifices open spiritual doorways, illustrating the dangers of tampering with unseen realms. Be warned: Following the images, visuals, and scenarios in shows like this can subtly spark a curiosity in the supernatural that the enemy of our souls is eager to exploit, drawing hearts and minds into fascination with darkness rather than fear of the Lord. Remain anchored in Christ, always!

CHAPTER 9

DELIVERANCE AND CLOSING DEMONIC PORTALS

THE REASON I stand so firmly in the ministry of deliverance is because I have personally experienced its transformative power. As a believer, I had begun walking with the Lord and ministering to others. I was encountering Him in meaningful ways. Yet, as I deepened my relationship with God, I realized there were areas within me that needed healing and deliverance.

I carried wounds from abandonment and loss in my early childhood. Growing up without a physical father present and lacking the spiritual guidance I desperately needed during my adolescence left deep voids in my soul. In my search for love and fulfillment, I had turned to ungodly practices that opened gates and portals in my life. Even as a believer, I found myself battling ungodly thoughts, addiction, lust, perversion, insecurity, anger, and rage.

I reached a point of desperation, crying out to the Lord: "How can I serve You now yet be overwhelmed by these thoughts and desires? How can I truly be free?" The Lord led me to the Gospels, where He revealed the necessity of deliverance and the importance of closing spiritual gates and portals.

One evening, alone in my bedroom, I knelt before the Lord and poured out my heart. I confessed the generational ties that I knew existed. I also laid at His feet the wounds and the openings in my soul that had given the enemy access. I asked the Lord to break and sever those ties, to uproot the deep-seated issues in my life. I pleaded with Him to close every gateway and portal that the enemy was using to torment me and to fill me with His Spirit like never before.

In that moment, the power of God descended upon me. I felt a release, as if chains were being broken and burdens were lifted. Those gates were closed, and I stepped into a victory that I had never experienced before. Since that encounter, I have never looked back. God delivered me in a powerful way! And then He equipped me to minister deliverance to others, helping them walk in the freedom that He so graciously gives. Praise be to God!

Deliverance is the process by which a person is set free from the influence or oppression of demonic forces. It is a powerful act of God's grace and authority, allowing believers to close any demonic portals that may have been opened in their lives and to reclaim their freedom in Christ. This chapter explores the biblical foundations of deliverance, including the steps involved in the process. We will also learn how to maintain freedom after deliverance.

The Biblical Foundation for Deliverance

Deliverance is a central theme in the Bible, beginning with the deliverance of the Israelites from slavery in Egypt and continuing through the ministry of Jesus Christ. During His earthly ministry, Jesus performed numerous acts of deliverance, casting out demons and freeing people from spiritual bondage. In Matthew 8:16, we read, "When evening came, many who were demon-possessed were brought to him, and he drove out the spirits with a word and healed all the sick." This report demonstrates Jesus' authority over demonic forces and His commitment to bringing freedom to those oppressed by the enemy.

Jesus not only performed deliverance, but He also empowered His disciples to do the same. In Luke 10:19, Jesus declared, "I have given you authority to trample on snakes and scorpions and to overcome all the power of the enemy; nothing will harm you." This authority was not limited to the first disciples. No, it is available to *all* believers who are filled with the Holy Spirit, even today! The Great Commission, found in Mark 16:15–18, includes the provision to cast out demons as part of the broader mission to spread the gospel: "And these signs will accompany those who believe: In my name they will drive out demons" (v. 17).

Deliverance is an expression of God's love and His desire for His people to live in freedom. It is through deliverance that the power of the enemy is broken and the influence of demonic portals is nullified, allowing believers to walk in the fullness of their identity in Christ.

In deliverance, people are set free from demonic oppression, but that is only the first step. We must also help them to be reconciled to God. The enemy's primary goal is to separate people from God, leading them into bondage and spiritual darkness. Through deliverance, believers are restored to their rightful place in God's kingdom, where they can fully experience the divine inheritance of being His sons and daughters. This ministry of reconciliation is at the heart of the gospel, as it reflects God's desire to bring His children back into a relationship with Him, free from the chains of sin and demonic influence.

Signs That Deliverance May Be Needed

While deliverance is not always necessary for every spiritual struggle, certain signs may indicate the need for deliverance. These signs often point to the presence of a demonic portal that has been opened and needs to be closed. Some common indicators include the following:

- **Persistent sinful patterns:** Struggling with habitual sin that feels impossible to overcome, despite efforts to repent and change, may indicate a need for deliverance. This could be related to addictions, compulsive behaviors, or recurring sinful thoughts. Such patterns suggest that the enemy has gained a foothold and is using the open portal to keep the individual in bondage.

- **Unexplained physical or emotional distress:**
  Chronic physical ailments, mental torment, or emotional instability with no clear medical cause may
  suggest demonic oppression. Symptoms such as
  intense fear, anxiety, depression, or self-harm can
  sometimes be linked to demonic influence. When
  traditional methods of treatment fail to bring relief,
  it may be necessary to consider the possibility of
  spiritual interference.

- **Spiritual blockages:** Difficulty engaging in spiritual activities, such as prayer, worship, or reading
  the Bible, can be a sign of spiritual interference
  from a demonic source. This interference often is
  experienced as a sense of heaviness, distraction, or
  an inability to connect with God. The enemy seeks
  to create a barrier between the individual and God,
  making it difficult for them to receive spiritual
  nourishment and guidance.

- **Involvement in the occult or sinful practices:** If
  you have engaged in occult practices, witchcraft, or
  any form of idolatry, a demonic portal has likely
  been opened. Even if these practices are in the past,
  they can still have lingering effects that require
  deliverance to close the portal fully. The enemy uses
  these activities to establish a stronghold in the individual's life, making it essential to renounce and
  break any ties with these practices.

- **Generational curses or patterns:** Repeated patterns of sin, failure, or spiritual bondage within a
  family line may indicate the presence of a generational curse or demonic influence that needs to be
  broken through deliverance. These generational issues

can perpetuate cycles of destruction and oppression, affecting multiple generations if not addressed.

Generational curses are spiritual strongholds that are passed down from one generation to the next, often as the result of unrepented sin or involvement in the occult by ancestors. These curses may show up in various ways, such as chronic illness, poverty, broken relationships, or addiction. Breaking these curses requires recognizing their existence, repenting on behalf of previous generations, and renouncing any agreements with the enemy. Through the power of Christ, these curses can be broken, allowing the individual and their descendants to experience freedom and restoration.

The Process of Deliverance

We began to gain some insight into this in chapters 2 and 8. Now let's go deeper. Deliverance is a process that involves several key steps, each of which is essential for successfully closing demonic portals and achieving lasting freedom.

1. **Repentance:** The first step in deliverance is repentance, which involves acknowledging any sin or behavior that may have opened the demonic portal, confessing it to God, and asking for His forgiveness. Repentance is crucial because it breaks the legal right the enemy has to oppress or influence a person. First John 1:9 assures us, "If we confess our sins, he is faithful and just and will forgive us our sins and purify us from all unrighteousness." Through repentance, you turn away from sin and realign yourself with God's will.

2. **Forgiveness:** Forgiveness is a critical part of the deliverance process. Unforgiveness can be a major hindrance to deliverance, as it gives the enemy a

foothold in your life. Jesus taught the importance of forgiveness in Matthew 6:14–15: "For if you forgive other people when they sin against you, your heavenly Father will also forgive you. But if you do not forgive others their sins, your Father will not forgive your sins." As part of deliverance, it is essential to forgive anyone who has wronged you and to ask God to heal any wounds caused by past hurts. Forgiveness breaks the chains of bitterness and resentment, allowing God's healing power to flow freely.

3. **Renunciation:** As discussed previously, after repentance, it is important to renounce any involvement with the occult, sinful practices, or demonic influences. Remember, renunciation is a verbal declaration that severs all ties with the enemy and no longer gives him any place in your life. This process may include breaking generational curses, rejecting any lies you have believed, and canceling any agreements or covenants made with the enemy, whether knowingly or unknowingly. Renunciation is a powerful step that cuts off the enemy's access and nullifies his authority in the individual's life.

4. **Casting out demons:** Once the legal rights of the enemy have been broken through repentance, renunciation, and forgiveness, the next step is to cast out any demons that may be present. Deliverance should be approached with prayer, the authority of Jesus' name, and sometimes the assistance of mature believers or ministers who are experienced in deliverance ministry. In Mark 16:17, Jesus declared, "In my name they will drive out demons." It is important to approach this step with faith, confidence in God's power, and a reliance on the

Holy Spirit's guidance. Those who minister deliverance should do so with sensitivity and care. It is important that they always keep the individual's well-being in mind, ensuring that the process is carried out in a way that honors God and brings true freedom.

5. **Being filled with the Holy Spirit:** After the deliverance, it is vital to invite the Holy Spirit to fill any areas of your life that were previously occupied by the enemy. This ensures that there is no space for the enemy to return to. Ephesians 5:18 encourages believers to be continually filled with the Spirit: "Do not get drunk on wine, which leads to debauchery. Instead, be filled with the Spirit." The Holy Spirit's presence provides protection and guidance, helping the individual maintain their freedom and grow in their relationship with God.

During and after the deliverance process, it is crucial to have spiritual covering—support and guidance from mature believers, pastors, or spiritual leaders. This covering provides protection and accountability, ensuring that the individual is not isolated and vulnerable to further attacks from the enemy. The support of a faith community is invaluable in helping the individual stay grounded in their faith, continue to grow spiritually through discipleship, and maintain the freedom they have gained through deliverance. Let's go deeper!

Leaving the Past Behind

It is important to "press on" in the things of God in order to maintain one's deliverance:

> Not that I have already attained, or am already perfected; but I press on, that I may lay hold of that for which Christ

Jesus has also laid hold of me. Brethren, I do not count myself to have apprehended; but one thing I do, forgetting those things which are behind and reaching forward to those things which are ahead, I press toward the goal for the prize of the upward call of God in Christ Jesus.

— Philippians 3:12–14, nkjv

In quantum physics, teleportation refers not to physically moving from one place to another but to transferring the *state* of a particle (its information) instantaneously across space. This happens through a phenomenon called quantum entanglement, where two particles are so deeply connected that changing one instantly changes the other, even if they are far apart. Furthermore, "time travel" in quantum physics suggests that time is not linear. Instead, past, present, and future may coexist as dimensions we can potentially access. Concepts like wormholes and Einstein's relativity indicate that time can bend, allowing for the possibility of movement between different points in time.

Having this understanding is so powerful, as we can see that God's creation and cosmic laws tell of spiritual truths. This is why Jesus taught in parables using natural examples to reveal spiritual mysteries. I know you're probably wondering, "What does all of this have to do with deliverance?" Stick with me. If you miss it, it's because you dismissed it!

The apostle Paul expressed his desire to press on toward what lay ahead, urging believers to "forget the former things." Dwelling on negative things in the past—whether it be past traumas or mistakes, guilt, shame, or condemnation—often causes people to revisit (spiritually travel to) those painful moments emotionally and spiritually, repeatedly reopening old wounds and causing a spiritual and quantum entanglement. This cycle leaves many bound and oppressed, unable to embrace fully the freedom available in Christ. The pain of past attacks often resurfaces and manifests in the present, perpetuating the very struggles believers seek to overcome.

Deliverance brings freedom. That's the good news! More work needs to take place afterward too, however, in maintaining that freedom. After deliverance, it is important to take steps to ensure that the demonic portal remains closed and that the enemy does not regain access. A great spiritual key is keeping our minds on the "now of God" and the promises of the future, not to go back to what we've been delivered from. I emphasize, once you have been delivered from something or someone, do everything not to go back.

> Do not remember the former things, nor consider the things of old. Behold, I will do a new thing, now it shall spring forth; shall you not know it? I will even make a road in the wilderness and rivers in the desert.
> —Isaiah 43:18–19, nkjv

The following steps will help you keep demonic doors closed and maintain the freedom you have received through Christ.

Guard your heart and mind. Be vigilant about what you allow into your life, whether through media, relationships, or activities. Proverbs 4:23 advises, "Above all else, guard your heart, for everything you do flows from it." Protecting your heart and mind from negative influences helps close the demonic portal and ensures that you remain spiritually healthy. This may involve setting boundaries and avoiding certain environments. You must make intentional choices about what you consume mentally and emotionally.

Stay rooted in God's Word. Regularly reading, studying, and meditating on Scripture helps keep your mind and heart aligned with God's truth. Psalm 119:105 says, "Your word is a lamp for my feet, a light on my path." The Word of God serves as a guide and a defense against the enemy's attacks. By immersing yourself in Scripture, you can renew your mind and fortify yourself against any attempts by the enemy to reestablish a foothold in your life.

Develop a strong prayer life. Prayer is essential for maintaining spiritual strength and protection. Regular communication with God keeps you connected to His presence and power. Ephesians 6:18 encourages believers to "pray in the Spirit on all occasions with all kinds of prayers and requests. With this in mind, be alert and always keep on praying for all the Lord's people." Through prayer, you can seek God's guidance and ask for His protection. You can also intercede for others. All of this will create a strong spiritual foundation that resists demonic influence.

Engage in worship and fellowship. Worship and fellowship with other believers help create an environment where the Holy Spirit is welcomed, while demonic influences are resisted. Hebrews 10:24–25 emphasizes the importance of gathering together: "And let us consider how we may spur one another on toward love and good deeds, not giving up meeting together, as some are in the habit of doing, but encouraging one another—and all the more as you see the Day approaching." Being part of a faith community provides encouragement *and* accountability, both of which are vital for sustaining your freedom and spiritual growth.

Live a life of holiness and obedience. Choosing to live a life that honors God in every area prevents the enemy from finding a foothold. First Peter 1:15–16 calls believers to holiness: "But just as he who called you is holy, so be holy in all you do; for it is written: 'Be holy, because I am holy.'" Holiness serves as a powerful defense against the enemy's attempts to regain access to your life. By committing to a lifestyle of obedience to God's Word, you can maintain the freedom you've received through deliverance.

Having accountability partners—trusted individuals who can support you in your spiritual journey—is crucial for maintaining freedom after deliverance. These partners can help you stay on track, encourage you when you face challenges, and pray with you when you need strength. They can also help you identify any areas where you might be vulnerable to the enemy's attacks, offering guidance and support as you continue to walk in your newfound freedom.

The Role of the Church in Deliverance

The church plays a vital role in the ministry of deliverance, especially for those seeking freedom from demonic oppression. Churches need to be equipped with the knowledge and spiritual authority to minister deliverance effectively.

Training and equipping

Pastors and mature laypersons should be trained in the biblical principles of deliverance and prepared to assist those in need. This training should include understanding the spiritual dynamics of deliverance, including how to discern when deliverance is needed. Then it's important to show how to conduct deliverance with sensitivity and wisdom. Believers should also be aware of the spiritual authority they have in Christ to command demons to leave and to close any demonic portals.

Creating a safe environment

The church should create an environment where people feel safe to seek help and where deliverance is approached with sensitivity and discernment. This involves being nonjudgmental about whatever comes up in a deliverance session. Confidentiality is imperative, as is offering support throughout the deliverance process and beyond. The goal is to create a space where individuals can experience God's love and power, free from fear or shame.

Prevention through teaching

Additionally, the church can help prevent the opening of demonic portals by teaching sound doctrine—and that should include a warning against the dangers of occult practices. From the pulpit, believers should be encouraged to have lifestyles of holiness and obedience to God's Word. By educating its congregation about spiritual warfare and the reality of the unseen realm, the church empowers believers to live victoriously and avoid the pitfalls that lead to demonic influence.

The church is called to be a beacon of hope and a place of refuge for those seeking deliverance. As the body of Christ, the church has the responsibility to extend the ministry of Jesus—setting the captives free and proclaiming the good news of salvation. When the church operates in its full authority, it becomes a powerful force against the kingdom of darkness, helping individuals and communities experience the freedom that is found in Christ alone.

Deliverance is a powerful expression of God's love and authority, providing a way for believers to close demonic portals and experience true freedom in Christ. By understanding the biblical foundation for deliverance and recognizing the signs that may be needed, we can determine when deliverance is needed. Following the steps involved in the process will bring freedom from the influence of the enemy and allow believers to reclaim their spiritual authority.

As we have mentioned, deliverance is not a onetime event. It's part of our ongoing journey of faith. Maintaining freedom requires vigilance, a strong connection with God through prayer and His Word, and a commitment to living a life that honors Him (Phil. 2:12). As believers walk in their newfound freedom, they are called to help others experience the same deliverance, sharing the truth of God's power over darkness and His desire for all to live in the light.

As you move forward in your spiritual journey, remember that you are not alone. God is with you, empowering you to overcome every challenge and walk in the fullness of His love and power. The freedom Christ has won for you is precious and worth guarding with all your heart. Embrace it and then share it with others, knowing that, in doing so, you are advancing God's kingdom on earth.

Activation Prayer

Heavenly Father, thank You for the victory I have in Jesus Christ. Thank You for Your love, which sets me free from the chains of darkness and reconciles me to You. Lord, I ask that You reveal any areas in my life where demonic portals may be open. I repent of any sin that may have opened a door to the enemy. I renounce and close those gates now through the power of Your name and nature.

Fill me with Your Holy Spirit, Lord, so that there is no room for the enemy to return. Strengthen me to walk in holiness and obedience, guarding my heart and mind against the schemes of the enemy. Surround me with Your protection, and guide me in Your truth.

Father, I pray for those who are still bound, that they may experience the deliverance that comes through Jesus Christ. Use me as an instrument of Your freedom and grace, bringing hope to other people in my life who need Your powerful touch.

Thank You for Your faithfulness and the freedom I have in You. I'm determined never to go back to the things and people You've delivered me from! I trust You to lead me in victory every day. In Jesus' mighty name, I pray. Amen.

DID YOU KNOW?

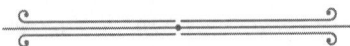

Trauma-focused therapies often emphasize the power of verbal confession in emotional healing. Similarly, in deliverance ministry, confessing and renouncing sin close demonic portals, breaking spiritual strongholds and restoring peace.

PORTALS IN POP CULTURE:
CERN and the Large Hadron Collider (2008–Present)

The world's largest and most powerful particle accelerator, located at the European Organization for Nuclear Research (CERN) in Switzerland, has sparked numerous theories that its experiments could open portals to other dimensions. While science presents it as exploration, spiritually discerning believers must ask, "What gates are being opened, and who or what has legal access through them?" In a time where both heaven and hell are seeking entry points into the earth, we are called to partner with God to open the gates of glory and shut down the gateways of darkness.

CHAPTER 10

WALKING IN AUTHORITY OVER PORTALS

THE LORD CALLED my family and me to minister in what is considered one of the most dangerous cities in America—a place burdened with poverty and crime. Despite the challenges, we knew God had a purpose for sending us there. He made it clear that we were to enter this region to "restore the walls." By doing so, we would reveal Christ to other people and manifest His power and hope.

As we entered this new city of divine assignment, we committed ourselves to prayer, intercession, evangelism, and discipling those in the community. Over time, longtime residents began to share remarkable stories with us. Many confessed that they had never seen their community in the way it was now.

This was once a place that bred fear, where drug dealing and prostitution were rampant, visible day and night. Yet something miraculous had happened. Through the power and authority of Christ, the entire spiritual climate had begun to shift.

Residents shared how the community, which once appeared cloaked in darkness, now seemed illuminated. They described how crime had decreased, including prostitution, and a sense of peace had filled the area. They would often say that the community now appeared filled with light.

This transformation was not the result of human effort alone, but it was made possible through the authority given to us in Christ Jesus. By His power, we closed demonic gates and opened portals of God's glory. This testimony serves as a reminder of the authority we hold in Christ to impact and transform even the darkest places.

As believers in Christ, we are called to walk in the authority that

God has given us over all spiritual forces, including the ability to open heavenly portals and close demonic ones. This authority is not something we earn or achieve on our own. It's a gift from God, granted through the work of Jesus Christ on the cross and empowered by the Holy Spirit. This chapter explores what it means to walk in spiritual authority and maintain it in our daily lives.

Understanding Spiritual Authority

Spiritual authority is the God-given right and power to govern and command in the spiritual realm. It is the ability to enforce the will of God by resisting the devil. In this practice, we influence the world for the kingdom of God. Jesus demonstrated this authority throughout His earthly ministry by healing the sick and casting out demons. In Matthew 28:18–20, after His resurrection, Jesus declared, "All authority in heaven and on earth has been given to me. Therefore go and make disciples of all nations, baptizing them in the name of the Father and of the Son and of the Holy Spirit, and teaching them to obey everything I have commanded you. And surely I am with you always, to the very end of the age."

Jesus' authority is now extended to every believer through the indwelling of the Holy Spirit. This means that as followers of Christ, we have the authority to open heavenly portals, inviting God's presence and blessings into our lives. We can also close demonic portals, shutting down the enemy's influence and activity.

This authority does not depend on our own strength or merit. It's based on our relationship with Christ. Ephesians 2:6 tells us that God "raised us up with Christ and seated us with him in the heavenly realms in Christ Jesus." Being seated with Christ in heavenly places signifies our position of authority in Him. We operate from a place of victory, not defeat, because Christ has already overcome the enemy. Understanding our identity in Christ is crucial to exercising spiritual authority effectively. When we know who we are in Christ, we can confidently step into the authority He has given us, knowing that it does not depend on our abilities but on His finished work on the cross.

To walk in authority over portals, we must first understand how to open them, inviting God's presence and power into our lives and circumstances. This opening requires an intentional effort to align ourselves with God's will and use the spiritual tools He has provided.

Prayer

Prayer is one of the most powerful ways to exercise spiritual authority and open heavenly portals. It is our way of communicating with the all-powerful Creator of the universe! When we pray, we declare and activate the promises He has given us in His Word, and we invite His intervention in our lives—not just to "get" the things we want. We have the privilege of aligning our hearts with His purposes as we pray, and then we can effectively release His will on the earth, just as it is in heaven. James 5:16 reminds us, "The prayer of a righteous person is powerful and effective." When we pray in faith, we activate the authority given to us in Christ, and heavenly portals are opened.

Worship

Worship creates an atmosphere where God's presence is welcomed and celebrated. As we worship, we open portals to heaven, allowing God's glory to fill our lives and environments. Psalm 95:1–2 instructs, "Come, let us sing for joy to the Lord; let us shout aloud to the Rock of our salvation. Let us come before him with thanksgiving and extol him with music and song." This invitation to collective worship emphasizes the joy and power found in praising God together.

Worship enthrones God in our midst, opening a portal for His power and blessings to flow. Worship is a powerful act of surrender and adoration, drawing us closer to God and inviting His presence to manifest in tangible ways.

Declaring God's Word

Speaking and declaring Scripture is another way to exercise authority and bring God's manifested presence from heaven and into the earth. God's Word is living and active, and when we declare it with faith, we align ourselves with His will and release His power into our situations. Isaiah 55:11 assures us, "So is my word that goes out from my mouth: It will not return to me empty, but will accomplish what I desire and achieve the purpose for which I sent it." By declaring God's Word, we open portals for His purposes to be fulfilled in our lives. Speaking Scripture over our lives and situations is an act of faith that releases God's promises and brings His kingdom into our reality.

Obedience

Obedience to God's commands is crucial in exercising spiritual authority. When we walk in obedience, we align ourselves with God's kingdom, which empowers us to open heavenly portals. In John 14:15, Jesus said, "If you love me, keep my commands." Obedience is a demonstration of our love for God and our submission to His authority, which, in turn, allows us to operate in the authority He has given us. Obedience is not about legalism, but it is about responding to God's love with a heart that desires to please Him and fulfill His purposes.

Faith is the foundation upon which spiritual authority is built. Hebrews 11:6 tells us that "without faith it is impossible to please God, because anyone who comes to him must believe that he exists and that he rewards those who earnestly seek him." Exercising authority over portals requires faith—faith in God's Word, faith in His promises, and faith in the power of the name of Jesus. When we step out in faith, even in the face of opposition, we activate the authority given to us and witness the realities of heaven breaking into our circumstances.

Exercising Authority to Close Demonic Portals

Just as we have the authority to open heavenly portals, we also have the authority to close demonic portals that the enemy may attempt to open in our lives. Closing them requires a proactive approach to spiritual warfare, recognizing the tactics of the enemy and taking decisive action to shut down his influence.

- **Resist the devil.** James 4:7 instructs us, "Submit yourselves, then, to God. Resist the devil, and he will flee from you." Resisting the devil involves standing firm in faith. When he tries to fill your mind with his lies, actively change your thoughts. Quote the promises of God to yourself. Absolutely refuse to give him any ground in your life! By resisting the devil, you close demonic portals and prevent him from gaining a foothold. This resistance is not passive but an active stance against the enemy's attempts to derail your life.

- **Bind and loose.** In Matthew 16:19, Jesus gave believers the authority to bind and loose: "I will give you the keys of the kingdom of heaven; whatever you bind on earth will be bound in heaven, and whatever you loose on earth will be loosed in heaven." Binding refers to restricting the enemy's activities, while loosing involves releasing God's will and purposes. By exercising this authority, you can shut down the work of the enemy and release the blessings and promises of God. Binding and loosing are acts of spiritual warfare that empower believers to take control of situations, align them with God's will, and shut down the enemy's operations.

- **Plead the blood of Jesus.** The blood of Jesus is one of the most powerful weapons we have in spiritual warfare. Revelation 12:11 tells us, "They triumphed over him by the blood of the Lamb and by the word of their testimony." Pray the blood of

Jesus over every aspect of your life and the lives of
those you love. Shut down the work of the enemy in
his tracks. The blood of Jesus cancels out any legal
claim the enemy might have had. The blood of
Jesus is the ultimate declaration of victory over the
enemy's plans for our lives, ensuring that we remain
under God's protection and authority.

Our testimonies serve as powerful tools in closing demonic
portals and defeating the enemy. Revelation 12:11 emphasizes the
importance of the word of our testimony in overcoming the devil.
By sharing the amazing things that God has done in our lives, we
not only encourage others to seek Him for the same, but we also
remind the devil of our victory! Testimonies remind us of God's
faithfulness and the power of His work in our lives, making it difficult for the enemy to regain a foothold.

Walking in spiritual authority must become a lifestyle that we
practice every day. Maintaining this authority requires a continual
commitment to live in alignment with God's will and to exercise
the authority He has given us regularly. To develop a lifestyle that
empowers us to walk in spiritual authority, we must do the following.

Commune with God daily. Regular time spent in prayer, worship, and reading God's Word strengthens our connection with
Him and reinforces our authority in the spiritual realm. Jesus set
the example of maintaining constant communion with the Father,
often withdrawing to pray (Luke 5:16). This regular communion
keeps us attuned to God's voice and His will. By prioritizing our
relationship with God, we remain sensitive to His leading and
empowered to exercise our authority effectively.

Walk in holiness and integrity. Living a life of holiness and
integrity is essential for maintaining spiritual authority. Sin and
compromise weaken our authority and give the enemy access to
our lives. First Peter 1:16 reminds us, "Be holy, because I am holy."
By striving to live holy lives, we protect our spiritual authority and

keep demonic portals closed. Holiness is not just about avoiding sin; it is about pursuing righteousness, reflecting God's character in our daily lives, and setting ourselves apart for His purposes.

Grow in spiritual discernment. Spiritual discernment is the ability to perceive the presence and activity of spiritual forces, both good and evil. It is crucial for recognizing when a demonic portal is being opened or when a heavenly portal needs to be activated. First Corinthians 12:10 identifies the discernment of spirits as a gift of the Holy Spirit. Cultivating this gift helps us navigate the spiritual realm effectively and exercise our authority with wisdom. Through discernment, we can respond appropriately to spiritual challenges, ensuring that we remain aligned with God's will and purpose.

Be bold in faith. Exercising spiritual authority requires boldness and confidence in God's power and promises. Hebrews 4:16 encourages us to "approach God's throne of grace with confidence, so that we may receive mercy and find grace to help us in our time of need." Boldness in faith enables us to take decisive action when confronting the enemy and to declare God's Word with authority. This boldness is rooted not in self-confidence but in trusting God's ability to work through us, even when faced with opposition.

Consistency in our spiritual practices is key to maintaining authority over portals. Just as physical fitness requires regular exercise, spiritual authority is strengthened and sustained through consistent prayer, worship, and study of the Word. Consistency builds spiritual muscle, enabling us to respond with authority when challenges arise. It also creates a habit of dependence on God, ensuring that our actions are always rooted in His power rather than our own.

Encouraging Others to Walk in Authority

As we grow in our understanding and practice of spiritual authority, we are called to encourage and equip others to do the same. Discipleship involves teaching others how to exercise their authority in Christ and helping them recognize their identity as children of God, who have been given power over the enemy.

- **Teaching and mentoring:** One of the most effective ways to encourage others to walk in authority is through teaching and mentoring. Sharing biblical principles, personal experiences, and practical applications can help others understand their spiritual authority and how to use it effectively. By imparting knowledge and wisdom, we can help others grow in confidence and competence in their spiritual walk.

- **Praying with others:** Praying with others, especially in times of need or spiritual attack, helps reinforce their faith and authority. By standing together in prayer, we can open heavenly portals and close demonic ones on behalf of those who may be struggling. Corporate prayer amplifies the power of individual faith, creating a spiritual synergy that can break through even the most stubborn barriers.

- **Modeling a life of authority:** Living out your spiritual authority in everyday life serves as a powerful example to others. When people see the fruit of walking in authority—such as peace, protection, and victory over challenges—they are encouraged to seek the same in their own lives. Your life becomes a testimony of God's power, inspiring others to step into their own authority and experience the fullness of what God has for them.

- **Encouraging collective authority:** When we encourage those around us to walk in the authority God has given to them, we are doing more than just helping those few people. As we all begin to exercise authority over the enemy together, we become a powerful force for God's kingdom! When believers come together in unity, exercising their authority as one body, the impact multiplies. The church becomes a force to be reckoned with, advancing God's kingdom and pushing back the forces of darkness in a powerful way.

Unity among believers enhances spiritual authority. Jesus emphasized the importance of unity in John 17:21, praying that all believers would be one, just as He and the Father are one. When the church operates in unity, the authority of each believer is magnified, and the collective impact is far greater than the sum of its parts. This unity doesn't mean mental agreement in every issue. But together, as we commit to following God together and spiritually aligning with His purposes, His power is multiplied, and miraculous things can happen!

Walking in authority over portals is an important aspect of the Christian life. It empowers us to bring the realities of heaven into our earthly experience and shut down the influence of the enemy. We can't "earn" this authority. It's given to us because of what the Lord Jesus did for us on the cross of Calvary.

As you continue to grow in your understanding of spiritual authority, remember that you are seated with Christ in heavenly places and that you operate from a position of victory. You have every right to exercise this authority! Pray and declare God's Word over your life. Refuse to settle for anything less than His best! When you do, you can consistently open heavenly portals and close demonic ones.

Remember this also: It's not all about you! When you exercise your spiritual authority, it can bring many benefits to your own life, which then overflow onto other people. As you walk in your authority, those around you are blessed! This outflow is part of your calling as a believer—to be a vessel through which God's kingdom is established on the earth.

Finally, always keep in mind that the authority you wield is rooted in your relationship with Jesus Christ. Stay close to Him and draw on His strength as you need it. The Holy Spirit will guide you as you learn to listen to His voice.

May you continue to grow in the knowledge and exercise of the authority that has been given to you, and may your life be marked by the continual opening of heavenly portals, bringing the presence and power of God into every situation you face.

Activation Prayer

Heavenly Father, thank You for the authority You have given me through Christ Jesus. Thank You for seating me in heavenly places and equipping me to walk in victory over the enemy. Lord, I ask for wisdom and discernment to recognize the spiritual forces at work around me.

Empower me to open heavenly portals that bring Your presence and power into every situation. Strengthen me to close demonic portals and resist the enemy's attempts to gain a foothold in my life.

Help me walk boldly in the authority You have given me, always relying on Your Spirit to guide and strengthen me. May my life reflect Your light and bring transformation to the people and places I encounter.

I pray for those who are struggling to recognize or exercise their authority. Lord, reveal their identity in You, and equip them to stand firm in faith. Let their lives be testimonies of Your power and goodness. In Jesus' mighty name, I pray. Amen.

DID YOU KNOW?

Studies on body language and posture show that confident stances reduce cortisol (the stress hormone) and increase testosterone (the dominance hormone), empowering individuals to feel more authoritative. Walking in spiritual authority also involves confidence in Christ, reflected in both spiritual and physical states.

PORTALS IN POP CULTURE:
The Stargate in *Stargate SG-1* (1997–2007 TV series)

In this sci-fi series, a portal device called the Stargate allowed travel to distant planets and dimensions. The idea of ancient civilizations using portals aligns with theories about spiritual gateways, bridging the gap between reality and the divine or demonic realms. Though fictional, the series serves as a cultural illustration of the real spiritual portals this book explores. Some open doors to heaven, others to darkness.

CHAPTER 11

CREATING A HEAVENLY PORTAL IN YOUR HOME

REMEMBER AN INSTANCE when I was ministering in West Virginia. Before leaving, I noticed that my daughter was becoming ill. Concerned, I spoke to my wife and asked her to monitor our daughter closely, keep her covered in prayer, and ensure she received the care she needed. My wife reassured me, releasing me to fulfill the ministry assignment God had given me.

Just minutes before I was to step onto the platform to minister, I received a phone call from my wife. She was panicking, explaining that our daughter's condition had worsened to the point where they were rushing her to the emergency room. She was in critical condition. As you can imagine, the human part of me became overwhelmed with worry. My heart sank, and I felt torn between my responsibility to minister to God's people and my deep concern for my daughter.

In that moment, I clung to the promises of God. I reminded myself that God would not send me on His assignment without also taking care of my family. I began to pray fervently, asking the Lord to heal my daughter. I needed His peace to determine what I needed to do and His strength to minister to the people despite the situation unfolding in my family. What happened next was nothing short of supernatural. Moments before stepping onto the stage, a peace I could not explain washed over me. Despite understanding my daughter's critical condition, I felt a divine strength rise within me to do the work of the Lord.

As I took the microphone to minister, I began to worship from the depths of my spirit. While leading the congregation in worship,

I envisioned my daughter and family covered in God's light. In a vision, I saw that light traveling to my daughter's side, bringing healing and restoration. The service was powerful, and God's presence manifested tangibly, touching many lives.

After the service, I quickly got in my car and drove to Washington, DC, where my daughter was hospitalized. As I drove, I cried tears of gratitude, knowing that God was already at work. Upon arriving at the hospital, I embraced my wife, and together we prayed and worshipped at our daughter's bedside. Though she was still in a critical state, we sensed a supernatural peace in that room.

We interceded as a family, lifting up our voices in prayer and declaring healing over her life. What should have been a dire situation turned into a testimony of God's miraculous power. Our daughter recovered, defying all medical expectations. It was a truly miraculous healing, a testament to the power of prayer and worship within a family.

This experience reaffirmed to me the importance of creating a heavenly portal in our homes. When we pray and worship together as a family, we can invite God's presence to work mightily, even in the most critical moments.

Our homes are more than just the physical spaces where we live. They are the spiritual environments in which we dwell, and we can either invite the presence of God there or allow negative influences to take root. As believers, we have the privilege and responsibility to create an atmosphere in our homes that welcomes God's presence and opens portals to His blessings. This chapter explores practical ways to cultivate a home environment that serves as a heavenly portal, filled with the presence of God.

The Importance of a God-Centered Home

The foundation of a heavenly portal in your home is a life centered on God. When a household puts Jesus in the center of everything, the atmosphere is transformed into one where heavenly portals can be consistently open. Proverbs 3:33 states, "The LORD's curse is on the house of the wicked, but he blesses the home of the righteous." A home that honors God is a place of blessing, where His favor resides.

Creating a God-centered home begins with establishing God as the head of the household. This involves making Him the central focus of daily life—not just in religious practices but in every decision, action, and interaction. Joshua 24:15 famously declares, "But as for me and my household, we will serve the LORD." This declaration should be the foundation upon which the atmosphere of the home is built, ensuring that everything aligns with God's will and purposes.

A God-centered home also reflects the values of the kingdom of God. This means cultivating an environment where love and forgiveness are practiced daily. When these values are present, they create a spiritual atmosphere that is conducive to God's presence and opens the door for heavenly encounters.

To cultivate a home that serves as a heavenly portal, it is essential to incorporate daily spiritual practices that invite God's presence and keep the spiritual atmosphere charged with His power.

Establishing regular prayer times in the home is crucial for creating an environment where God's presence is felt. First Thessalonians 5:17 encourages believers to "pray continually." Consistent prayer keeps the lines of communication with God open and maintains a heavenly portal in the home. Family prayer, in particular, holds great power, as it unites the household in seeking God's guidance and protection.

Create a family prayer altar

Consider designating a specific place in your home as a family prayer altar, where everyone can gather for prayer. This space can be simple—a corner of a room, a table with a Bible, or a place where you perceive the manifest presence of God. By having a dedicated space for prayer, you reinforce the importance of seeking God together as a family, and the place becomes a physical reminder of your commitment to making Him the center of your home.

Regularly meditate on and discuss Scripture

The Word of God is a powerful tool for opening heavenly portals. Regularly reading, meditating on, and discussing Scripture within the household fills the home with God's truth and aligns the hearts and minds of those living there with His will. Deuteronomy 6:6–9 emphasizes the importance of keeping God's Word central in the home: "These commandments that I give you today are to be on your hearts. Impress them on your children. Talk about them when you sit at home and when you walk along the road, when you lie down and when you get up. Tie them as symbols on your hands and bind them on your foreheads. Write them on the doorframes of your houses and on your gates."

You can incorporate Scripture into your daily life by placing Bible verses in visible areas around your home. Many people love to hang beautiful pictures with Scriptures on the wall, but writing them on your bathroom mirror or putting notes with Bible verses on the fridge works just as well. These verses serve as constant reminders of God's promises and help to keep your focus on Him throughout the day. Additionally, consider making Scripture reading a part of your family's daily routine, such as during meals or before bedtime. This practice helps to create a continuous flow of God's Word in your home, keeping the heavenly portal open and active.

Spend time in worship

Colossians 3:16 tells us, "Let the message of Christ dwell among you richly as you teach and admonish one another with all wisdom through psalms, hymns, and songs from the Spirit, singing to God with gratitude in your hearts." Worship invites God's presence into the home. Playing worship music in the background as you cook dinner or singing songs of praise in the car creates an atmosphere of gratitude and reverence for God that can open heavenly portals and usher in His presence. Worship creates a dwelling place for Him within the home.

Worship is more than just singing or playing music on a Sunday morning. Did you know you can worship the Lord even in your daily routines? For example, you can worship God through your work by offering it to Him as an act of service or by expressing gratitude for the simple blessings in life. When worship becomes a lifestyle, your home becomes a continual portal for God's presence, as every action and moment become an opportunity to honor Him.

Periodically cleansing the home of any objects that do not honor God is important for maintaining a heavenly portal. This cleansing may involve removing items associated with occult practices or sinful activities, or it could be as simple as dealing with any lingering negative emotions or conflicts within the household. Acts 19:19 provides a biblical example of this practice, where new believers in Ephesus brought their scrolls of magic and burned them publicly as an act of renunciation.

Spiritually cleanse your home

A spiritual cleansing of your home can be a powerful act of dedication to God. Prayerfully walk through each room, asking the Holy Spirit to reveal anything that may not be pleasing to Him. As you identify these items or influences, remove or destroy them, and invite God's presence to fill the space. Consider praying and anointing the entrances to your home with oil as a symbolic act of dedication and protection, marking your home as a place where only God's presence is welcome.

Peace is one of the hallmarks of a home that serves as a heavenly portal. The Bible describes peace as a gift from God, one that transcends understanding and guards the hearts and minds of believers (Phil. 4:7). To create a peaceful environment in your home, it's important to develop a culture of love and forgiveness. You can do that by resolving conflicts quickly and promoting love and unity. Work to understand each other deeply, and be quick to ask for forgiveness when you have wronged someone in the household.

Unresolved conflict can create an atmosphere of tension and hinder the flow of God's presence in the home. Ephesians 4:26–27 advises, "In your anger do not sin: Do not let the sun go down while you are still angry, and do not give the devil a foothold." Addressing issues promptly and seeking reconciliation help maintain peace and keep the heavenly portal open. Open communication and a willingness to forgive are essential to preserving the peace and unity of the household.

In addition, having unity within the household is vital for creating a heavenly portal. Psalm 133:1 says, "How good and pleasant it is when God's people live together in unity!" Encourage family members to support one another, speak kindly, and demonstrate love in their actions. When a household is united in love, it creates an environment where God's presence can dwell richly.

Fostering unity in your home can be as simple as sharing meals together, spending quality time with one another, and making an effort to understand each other's perspectives. Family meetings or devotions can also effectively address any issues as they arise and ensure everyone is on the same page spiritually. When unity is prioritized, the home becomes a stronger portal for God's blessings and presence.

Actively inviting God's peace into your home can be done through prayer and the declaration of Scripture. For example, you can pray over your home, asking God to fill it with His peace, and declare verses like John 14:27, where Jesus said, "Peace I leave with you; my peace I give you. I do not give to you as the world gives. Do not let your hearts be troubled and do not be afraid." This covering invites a sense of calm and security into the household, ensuring that the home remains a heavenly portal.

There are also practical steps you can take to bring a peaceful atmosphere in your home. Try reducing excess clutter or organizing spaces, especially those you use most often. Consider painting your walls or decorating with calming colors, or light some pleasant-smelling candles to bring a peaceful and pleasant atmosphere into your home. These physical changes can contribute to an environment that feels restful and welcoming, making it easier for everyone in the household to experience God's peace. Furthermore, limiting noise and distractions during times of prayer or devotion can help maintain a focused and peaceful atmosphere conducive to encountering God.

Generosity is another way to extend the blessings of a heavenly portal. You could give to your church or share your time and resources with others, as generosity opens the door for God's provision to flow. Proverbs 11:25 states, "A generous person will prosper; whoever refreshes others will be refreshed." A home characterized by generosity reflects the nature of God and keeps the heavenly portal open for continued blessings.

We should be generous on a regular basis, making it part of a lifestyle of worship that permeates every aspect of our homes and interactions. A generous person is eager to give in many different ways! When generosity becomes a natural outflow of your life, it creates a ripple effect that touches everyone you encounter, making your home a beacon of God's love and provision.

Protecting the Spiritual Atmosphere of Your Home

Once you have established a heavenly portal in your home, it is important to protect it. The enemy will often seek to disrupt the peace and spiritual atmosphere of a home that honors God. Here are some practical ways to safeguard your home:

Be mindful of what you allow in your home. What you allow into your home—through media, entertainment, or even conversations—can either invite God's presence or open the door to negative influences. Philippians 4:8 encourages believers to focus on things that are true, noble, right, pure, lovely, admirable, excellent, and praiseworthy. Ensuring that these values are reflected in your home helps maintain a positive spiritual atmosphere.

Set boundaries for what is allowed in your home. This is crucial for protecting the spiritual atmosphere. It may involve being selective about the movies, music, and television shows that are watched, as well as the type of content that is accessed on social media platforms. Encouraging positive, uplifting, and faith-based media can help reinforce the values you want to cultivate in your home, keeping the heavenly portal open and the environment free from negative influences.

Pray regularly for God's protection over your home and family. Ask Him to place a hedge of protection around your home, safeguarding it from spiritual attacks or negative influences. Psalm 34:7 is a powerful verse to declare over your home, as it speaks of God's protection and His promise to guard those who fear and serve Him.

In addition to prayer, you can take practical steps to protect your home spiritually. Anoint your door frames with oil as you pray and invite God's presence on all those who enter your space. Again, you can place Scripture verses in visible locations throughout your house, and have regular family devotions to keep everyone focused on God's covering and protection. Inviting the Holy Spirit to fill your home daily creates a strong spiritual barrier against any attempts by the enemy to disrupt the peace and sanctity of your home.

One of the greatest privileges and responsibilities the Lord has given me as a spiritual priest, husband, and father is leading my family in Communion (the Lord's Supper) weekly at home. It has become a powerful gateway to God's manifest presence. This is a practice you can adopt to invite God's blessings into your household (Matt. 26:26–28; 1 Cor. 11:23–26).

Stay committed to the spiritual practices that keep the heavenly portal open. Regular prayer, worship, and Bible reading should continue to be a priority, even when life gets busy. These disciplines keep the spiritual atmosphere of your home strong and resistant to any attempts by the enemy to disrupt it.

Consistency in spiritual discipline is key to maintaining the authority and protection of your home. Just as physical exercise strengthens the body, regular spiritual practices strengthen your home's spiritual atmosphere. Encourage every member of your household to participate in these practices, creating a collective commitment to keeping the heavenly portal open and ensuring that your home remains a sanctuary of God's presence.

Your Home as a Spiritual Legacy

Remember that your home is more than just a physical space. It's a spiritual sanctuary where God's presence can be experienced and shared with all those who enter. As you commit to maintaining a heavenly portal in your home, you will see the blessings of God flow into the lives of everyone who enters your home. Moreover, by creating such an environment, you are establishing a spiritual legacy for future generations—a legacy that reflects the values of God's kingdom and invites His presence to continue dwelling in your family line.

As you embark on the journey of creating and maintaining a heavenly portal in your home, rest assured that God is with you every step of the way. He desires to fill your home with His presence that can change the lives of everyone there. His peace and power will fill your dwelling, and as you seek Him, He will faithfully guide you. Let your home be a place where His kingdom is made manifest, where the love of God and the joy of the Lord abound! There God's light will shine brightly for all to see.

May your home be a place filled with divine encounters—a true reflection of heaven on earth.

Creating a heavenly portal in your home is one of the most impactful things you can do as a believer. By establishing a God-centered environment, incorporating daily spiritual practices, promoting peace and unity, and extending hospitality and generosity, you invite God's presence to dwell richly in your home.

Activation Prayer

Heavenly Father, I thank You for the gift of our homes and the opportunity to make them places where Your presence dwells. Lord, I dedicate my home to You, inviting You to fill every room with Your peace. Help me create an atmosphere that honors You, where heavenly portals are consistently open, allowing Your blessing, protection, and provision to flow freely.

Teach me to prioritize You in every area of my life and to cultivate daily spiritual practices that draw me closer to You. May my times of prayer and worship serve as pillars that keep my home centered on You.

I ask for Your guidance in fostering unity and peace within my household. Help us love and forgive easily, supporting one another and reflecting the values of Your kingdom. May my home be a sanctuary of hope and healing, a place where others can encounter the reality of Christ.

Protect my home from any negative influences, and guard our family's hearts and minds as we seek to honor You in all that we do. Let my home be filled with light, love, and the power of Your Spirit.

I give You all the glory and praise, trusting You to guide me in this journey. May my home always be a reflection of heaven on earth. In Jesus' powerful name, I pray. Amen.

DID YOU KNOW?

Research on environmental psychology shows that cluttered or chaotic spaces increase stress, while clean, peaceful environments promote calmness and creativity. Spiritually, creating a God-centered home invites heavenly peace and protects against negative influences.

PORTALS IN POP CULTURE:
The Skinwalker Ranch in Utah

Known for strange phenomena, the Skinwalker Ranch has been the subject of numerous studies and documentaries. Reports of UFOs, interdimensional sightings, and supernatural occurrences have led many to believe the site contains a portal to another realm. While the intrigue is strong, believers must exercise discernment, knowing spaces like these may be more than mysterious; they can be spiritual gateways the enemy uses to deceive, distract, and gain access. Remain in the Spirit!

CHAPTER 12

THE ROLE OF THE CHURCH IN OPENING HEAVENLY PORTALS

DURING ONE SIGNIFICANT season of ministry, we found ourselves gathering for our annual leadership retreat. The timing of this retreat coincided with Yom Kippur, the Day of Atonement on the Jewish calendar—a day marked by repentance of the people and God's forgiveness and restoration. This alignment was not planned by human hands. It was clearly orchestrated by God's sovereignty.

The atmosphere at this retreat felt different from the outset. There was a collective sense among the leadership team that we had entered into a new spiritual season. One of the team members articulated it beautifully, saying, "It feels like there has been a new birth." It was hard to explain, but everyone seemed to perceive that God was doing something extraordinary in our midst.

When it was my turn to share and teach, I approached the platform intending to impart instruction and encouragement, as I had done many times before. Yet, as I closed my eyes to pray, I was immediately overcome by the tangible presence of God. I began to weep uncontrollably in His glory.

Within me, there was a tension: My human side wanted to stick to the program, to move forward with the planned teaching. But my spirit knew better. I was caught between two decisions—follow the schedule or lean into what God was doing.

The leadership team, seated before me, seemed to sense my inner wrestling. They watched in anticipation as I chose to obey the Spirit's leading. Instead of teaching, I began to sing the hymn

"To God Be the Glory." As I worshipped, I called everyone to bow before the Lord in repentance and humility, thanking Him for what He was doing among us. What began as a simple moment of worship turned into a divine encounter.

The altar was flooded with people. We worshipped deeply, and the presence of God grew more intense. I fell to my knees, and though I was physically present, I entered a trance-like state. In this spiritual encounter, I saw an angel of the Lord carrying what looked and smelled like wine. The angel poured this wine, signifying the new wine of the Spirit that God was pouring out over the ministry.

For two hours, the sanctuary became a place of supernatural visitation. People were weeping as they worshipped God, and He was pouring out divine healing and deliverance upon them. Angels were ministering among us, and many testified to their encounters with the Lord. Some spoke of feeling waves of electricity coursing through their bodies as they were touched by the Spirit.

At one point, completely immersed in the Spirit, I found myself asking everyone to remove their shoes. As I laid hands on the feet of the people there, the Lord revealed that this act symbolized anointing their feet for the journey ahead—a commissioning for the new season we had entered.

When the encounter ended, the leaders recounted their own transformative experiences. They spoke of being surrounded by light, touched by God's power, and filled with renewed purpose. We all knew the ministry had crossed a threshold into a new season—a season marked by the outpouring of the new wine of the Spirit. All glory, honor, and praise to the living Christ!

The church, as the body of Christ, plays a pivotal role in opening portals into heaven and bringing the presence of God into the world. When believers gather together to worship the Lord truly, the corporate anointing they carry creates powerful spiritual gateways that allow God's glory to manifest in extraordinary ways. This chapter explores how the church can actively participate in opening heavenly portals that manifest the power of God into the earth.

The Church as a Gateway to Heaven

The church is often referred to as the "house of God," a place where heaven and earth meet. In Matthew 16:18–19, Jesus declared, "And I tell you that you are Peter, and on this rock I will build my church, and the gates of Hades will not overcome it. I will give you the keys of the kingdom of heaven; whatever you bind on earth will be bound in heaven, and whatever you loose on earth will be loosed in heaven." This passage underscores the authority given to the church to open and close spiritual portals, influencing the flow of God's will on the earth.

The church's role as a gateway to heaven goes beyond a mere gathering place for believers. It is an active conduit of divine power, where the spiritual authority given by Christ is exercised to bring about God's purposes on the earth. The concept of the church as a gateway implies that it is a place where the boundaries between heaven and earth are thin, where God's presence can be felt tangibly, and where the miraculous becomes possible.

In this context, the church is called to be more than a place of worship—it is to be a place of encounter, where individuals come face-to-face with the living God. It is where men and women of God proclaim the Word and God's people meet together for prayer and worship. It is also where we receive the sacraments. Yes, a Bible-believing church opens portals that allow the realities of heaven—such as healing, deliverance, and divine wisdom—to break into the natural world. The church's responsibility is to steward these moments of divine encounter, ensuring that they lead to lasting transformation in the lives of believers and the broader community.

Corporate Worship and the Manifestation of God's Presence

Corporate worship is one of the most powerful ways the church opens heavenly portals. When believers come together to worship in the Spirit and in truth, God's presence is specially drawn to the assembly.

> How good and pleasant it is when God's people live together in unity! It is like precious oil poured on the head, running down on the beard, running down on Aaron's beard, down on the collar of his robe. It is as if the dew of Hermon were falling on Mount Zion. For there the LORD bestows his blessing, even life forevermore.
>
> —PSALM 133:1–3

What power there is when we unite in worship to attract God's blessing and presence! When the church gathers to worship, we create a throne for God's presence, opening a portal for His glory to descend.

Corporate worship differs significantly from individual worship in its ability to amplify the spiritual atmosphere. The unity we experience together in worship creates a cumulative effect, building an environment that is highly conducive to the manifestation of God's presence. The early church experienced this dynamic on the day of Pentecost, as described in Acts 2. As the believers gathered in one place with one accord, their unified worship opened a portal to heaven, resulting in the outpouring of the Holy Spirit.

This principle of corporate worship opening portals is not just a historical fact that happened in Bible times. It can happen to those of us in the church today! When the church prioritizes corporate worship, it creates a consistent atmosphere that welcomes God's presence and releases His power. This kind of worship impacts all of us who are present, but it can even extend beyond the walls of the local church, affecting the entire community!

In modern times, we have seen the power of corporate worship to open portals and bring revival. Movements like the Toronto Blessing, the Brownsville Revival, and, more recently, the worship gatherings at Asbury University in Kentucky have demonstrated how sustained corporate worship can lead to widespread spiritual renewal. These movements have been marked by extended periods of worship, where the focus on God's presence has opened portals that have brought healing, deliverance, and revival to thousands.

The Power of Unity in Opening Portals

Unity within the church is crucial for opening heavenly portals. When believers are truly united, the power of their collective worship and prayer is amplified. Jesus emphasized the importance of unity in Matthew 18:19–20, saying, "Again, truly I tell you that if two of you on earth agree about anything they ask for, it will be done for them by my Father in heaven. For where two or three gather in my name, there am I with them." Unity invites God's presence and creates a portal for His will to be done on the earth.

Unity in the church is not just about avoiding conflict or resolving petty differences. It is so much more than that. When believers align their hearts and minds with God's purposes, this union creates a powerful synergy that can open portals to heaven in ways that individual efforts cannot. The early church understood this truth well, as seen in Acts 2:42–47, where the believers were of one heart and mind, sharing everything they had and praising God together. Their unity created an environment where miracles were commonplace, and the church grew rapidly.

In today's church, maintaining unity is more challenging than ever. We have so many differences that go far beyond doctrine, including controversies surrounding our culture today and even personal conflicts among church members. However, the church needs to strive for unity, recognizing that division weakens its spiritual power and hinders the opening of heavenly portals. Leaders must work diligently to foster an environment of love and respect, where every member feels valued and heard. When the church is united, it becomes a formidable force for the kingdom, capable of opening portals that bring God's presence into the world in transformative ways.

One of the keys to maintaining unity in the church is the practice of reconciliation. The Bible teaches that unresolved conflict can hinder our prayers and block the flow of God's blessings (Matt. 5:23–24). Therefore, the church must prioritize reconciliation, ensuring that any disagreements or offenses are dealt with quickly and biblically. When we work to preserve the unity in the church, we keep the portals to heaven open, allowing God's presence to flow freely.

Prayer and Intercession as Portal Openers

Corporate prayer and intercession are key activities the church engages in that open up a path for God's glory to be revealed. When the church prays together, aligning its will with God's, it exercises the authority given by Christ to bind and loose, opening the way for God's plans to be fulfilled on the earth. Acts 12:5–10 provides an example of the power of corporate prayer. When Peter was imprisoned, "the church was earnestly praying to God for him." As a result, a heavenly portal was opened, and an angel of the Lord appeared, freeing Peter from his chains and leading him out of the prison.

Intercession goes beyond simply praying for needs; it involves standing in the gap for others, for communities, and even for nations. The church's role as an intercessor is vital for opening portals that bring about significant spiritual breakthroughs. In 2 Chronicles 7:14, God has promised that if His people humble themselves, pray, and seek His face, He will hear from heaven and heal their land. This promise highlights the power of intercession to open portals that can lead to national healing and revival.

Intercessory prayer can take many forms, from small groups of dedicated prayer warriors to large-scale prayer gatherings that bring together thousands of believers. Each form of intercession has the potential to open heavenly portals, depending on the level of faith and how unified the people are with one another and with

God's will. The key is for the church to recognize the importance of intercession and to invest time and resources into cultivating a strong prayer ministry.

Throughout history, there have been powerful movements of intercession that have opened portals to heaven, leading to significant spiritual and societal changes. One such example is the Moravian Prayer Movement, which began in 1727 and continued uninterrupted for more than one hundred years. This movement opened portals that sustained a powerful revival among the Moravians, a revival that had a global impact that actually fueled the modern missionary movement, bringing thousands of people to the Lord.

Similarly, the 24/7 Prayer Movement, which started in the late twentieth century, has opened portals through continuous prayer, leading to spiritual renewal in countless communities around the world. These examples demonstrate the lasting impact that sustained corporate intercession can have when aligned with God's purposes.

The Impact of Open Portals on the Church and the World

When the church successfully opens heavenly portals, the impact is felt both within the church community and in the world at large. These open portals can bring about revival and transformation in people's lives. The tangible presence of God will change lives and alter the course of history!

Revival is often the direct result of open heavenly portals. When God's presence is welcomed into the church through unity in the worship and prayer of the people, it creates a spiritual environment that is ripe for revival. During times of revival, the normal order of things is disrupted as the presence of God becomes the central focus. Lives are transformed, and communities are renewed. The effects often ripple out to touch entire regions or nations.

When heavenly portals are open, the supernatural becomes a regular occurrence in the life of the church. Miracles of healing and deliverance will commonly take place. Prophetic revelation will guide people's lives. The manifestations of the Holy Spirit become common, drawing people to God and confirming His power and love. The early church experienced this phenomenon, as recorded in Acts 5:15–16, where people brought the sick into the streets, hoping that Peter's shadow might fall on them as he passed by: "Crowds gathered also from the towns around Jerusalem, bringing their sick and those tormented by impure spirits, and all of them were healed." This level of divine intervention is possible when the church consistently opens heavenly portals as the people pray and worship God in unity.

These supernatural manifestations certainly benefit the people present in the church. But they also serve as a powerful testimony to an unbelieving world! When the church operates in the supernatural, it demonstrates that the God of the Bible is alive and active today, capable of meeting the deepest needs of humanity. Miracles and healings often serve as the catalyst for evangelism, as they provide undeniable evidence of God's power and love, drawing people to faith in Christ.

The impact of open heavenly portals extends beyond the church walls, leading to the transformation of entire communities and societies. When the presence of God is welcomed into a region, it brings about changes that affect every aspect of life. Crime rates can decrease, and justice can be pursued more effectively. Social issues, like poverty and addiction, can be addressed with renewed vigor and divine guidance.

One historical example of this kind of transformation is the Welsh Revival of 1904–1905. As heavenly portals were opened through intense prayer and worship, the presence of God swept across Wales, leading to widespread repentance and spiritual renewal. The revival had a profound impact on society: Pubs closed due to a lack of business, crime rates dropped, and communities experienced unprecedented peace and unity. This transformation demonstrates that when the church successfully opens and sustains heavenly portals, the effects can be felt on a societal level, bringing about lasting change.

Open heavenly portals also play a crucial role in advancing the kingdom of God on a global scale. As the church prays and intercedes, these portals can facilitate the spread of the gospel to unreached people groups, support the work of missionaries, and help overcome spiritual strongholds in various regions. The global prayer movements that have arisen in recent decades, such as the Global Day of Prayer and the International House of Prayer in Kansas City, have opened portals that fuel missions, evangelism, and church-planting efforts around the world.

These global efforts are a fulfillment of Jesus' command in Matthew 28:19–20 to "go and make disciples of all nations, baptizing them in the name of the Father and of the Son and of the Holy Spirit, and teaching them to obey everything I have commanded you." As the church opens and sustains these portals, it helps bring the reality of God's kingdom to every corner of the earth, fulfilling the Great Commission.

The Church's Responsibility in Sustaining Open Portals

Once a heavenly portal is opened, the church has the responsibility to sustain it. The people must be committed to seeking God and walking in His holiness. Sustaining an open portal requires vigilance and dedication, as the enemy will often try to disrupt or close portals that are bringing significant change.

The church must remain steadfast in prayer, even when results are not immediately visible. Colossians 4:2 encourages believers to "devote yourselves to prayer, being watchful and thankful." Perseverance in prayer keeps the portal open and ensures that God's purposes continue to be fulfilled. This kind of perseverance requires faith and patience, trusting that God is at work even when the results are not yet apparent. The church must cultivate a culture of persistent, faith-filled prayer that continually presses into God's presence and intercedes for His will to be done on earth.

Regular corporate worship and a commitment to unity help maintain the spiritual atmosphere that keeps the portal open. Ephesians 4:3 urges believers to "make every effort to keep the unity of the Spirit through the bond of peace." By prioritizing worship and unity, the church creates a continuous flow of God's presence. This involves more than just going to church every week and then going back home. We must create a lifestyle of worship among all people and encourage relationships that build up rather than tear down.

The church must be intentional about addressing any issues that could disrupt unity, such as gossip, unforgiveness, or doctrinal disputes. By promoting a culture of love and mutual submission, the church can protect the unity that is essential for sustaining open heavenly portals.

The church must also uphold holiness and obedience to God's Word as a means of sustaining open portals. In 1 Peter 1:15–16, believers are called to live holy lives, reflecting the character of God. When the church lives in obedience and purity, it creates an environment where heavenly portals can remain open and effective. Holiness involves setting ourselves apart for God's purposes and avoiding anything that could defile or distract us from His will. It requires a commitment to personal and corporate purity, rejecting sin and embracing righteousness in every area of life.

Obedience is closely linked to holiness, as it involves aligning our actions with God's commands. Jesus said in John 14:15, "If you love me, keep my commands." The church must prioritize obedience to God's Word, ensuring that its teachings and practices are grounded in Scripture. By doing so, the church maintains its spiritual authority and keeps the portals open for God's presence to flow.

Finally, the church must remain vigilant against spiritual attack. The enemy will often attempt to close or disrupt open portals by sowing discord among us. He uses deception, and he distracts us with the problems of daily life to keep church members' focus off the Lord. Leaders and members alike must be aware of these tactics and respond with spiritual discernment and authority. Ephesians 6:11 encourages believers to "put on the full armor of God, so that you can take your stand against the devil's schemes." By staying spiritually alert and equipped, the church can protect the portals it has opened and continue to advance God's kingdom.

> Even them I will bring to My holy mountain, and make them joyful in My house of prayer. Their burnt offerings and their sacrifices will be accepted on My altar; for My house shall be called a house of prayer for all nations.
> —ISAIAH 56:7, NKJV

The church has a profound role in opening and sustaining heavenly portals. It is our mission to bring the presence and power of God into the world. We are called on a holy mission to create spiritual gateways that transform lives, communities, and even nations. As the body of Christ, we are called to steward these portals with care, ensuring that they remain open and continue to bring God's kingdom to the earth.

The responsibility of the church in this regard is both a privilege and a mandate. It requires a deep commitment to God's purposes, a willingness to work together in unity, and a dedication to living lives that reflect the holiness and love of Christ. When the church embraces this calling, it becomes a powerful instrument of God's will, capable of opening portals that change the world.

As you reflect on the role of the church in opening heavenly portals, consider how you can contribute to this mission. Whether through prayer, worship, intercession, or simply living a life that honors God, each believer has a part to play in creating an environment where God's presence is welcome and His power is released. May the church rise to its calling, united in purpose and empowered by the Holy Spirit, to open heavenly portals that change the world for the glory of God.

Activation Prayer

Heavenly Father, I thank You for the privilege of being part of Your church, a conduit for Your glory and presence on the earth. Lord, I ask that You empower us as Your unified body to open heavenly portals through our worship and prayer. Fill our gatherings with Your Spirit, and let Your glory dwell richly among us.

Teach us to surrender fully to Your leading, even when it requires stepping out of our comfort zones. Help us remain sensitive to Your presence and obedient to Your voice, creating spaces where You can move freely.

Lord, pour out the new wine of Your Spirit upon us. Restore us to You and transform us as individuals and as Your church. Anoint our feet for the journey ahead, and equip us to carry Your presence into the world. May we be vessels of Your love and power in a world that needs You so desperately.

We dedicate ourselves to You and Your purposes, trusting that You will guide us as we walk in Your ways. Let Your will be done on earth as it is in heaven.

In the mighty name of Jesus, I pray. Amen.

DID YOU KNOW?

Collective prayer has been shown to synchronize brain activity among participants, creating a sense of unity and shared purpose. This physiological effect mirrors the spiritual reality of the church as a unified body opening heavenly portals.

PORTALS IN POP CULTURE:
Visions of Heaven During Near-Death Experiences

Many people who have had near-death experiences report seeing a bright light or hearing angelic voices, as well as describe an overwhelming sense of peace. These accounts suggest glimpses into heavenly portals that bridge the physical and spiritual realms.

CHAPTER 13

GUARDING AGAINST DECEPTION

RECALL A PARTICULAR instance involving a young man who had been deeply blessed by God and was actively serving in ministry. He was someone I had prayed for, prophesied over, and seen grow tremendously in his walk with the Lord. But over time, I noticed he began to fade into isolation, withdrawing and disengaging from the ministry.

It was disheartening to see him pull away, especially since he had shown such promise. Others in the ministry tried reaching out to him, encouraging him to return and reconnect, but their attempts were met with resistance. At that moment, I knew that this battle wasn't one to be fought with words or persuasion. The Holy Spirit instructed me not to approach him directly but instead to enter a season of intercession for his soul.

As I prayed, the Holy Spirit began to reveal what was happening. The young man had been surrounded by individuals who were feeding him lies about my character and the ministry. They accused me of being a false teacher and claimed I engaged in ungodly practices. These deceptive arrows were designed to sever his connection to the ministry, the place to which he was supposed to be spiritually assigned and aligned, and, ultimately, to derail God's purposes for his life.

I continued to pray fervently for him, trusting that God would intervene. After some time, I noticed him attending services again—first one, then another. By the third service, he approached me, requesting a one-on-one conversation. I knew this was the moment God had prepared.

As we spoke, the young man broke down in tears. He confessed that he had been influenced by the lies and accusations of others. He admitted that he had started to believe these false claims about my character but that, during the time of his absence, the Holy Spirit had been working on his heart.

God Himself had revealed the truth to him. The Holy Spirit had shown him my character directly, beyond the distortions and deceptions he had been told. The young man shared that he now understood the enemy's strategy. The lies were meant to remove him from his spiritual community, which would have ultimately led to his disconnection from his calling, his destiny, and God's purposes for his life.

At that moment, I forgave him completely. We prayed together, breaking every lie and stronghold of the enemy. He was restored and filled with God's love and truth. Today, this young man is on fire for God! He is actively walking in the calling God has given to him and living out his destiny. His testimony is a powerful reminder of the importance of guarding against deception and staying anchored in God's truth.

In the spiritual realm, one of the enemy's most effective strategies is deception. Deception can lead believers away from the truth of God's Word, causing them to open demonic portals unknowingly or miss out on the blessings available through heavenly portals. As the Bible warns, even the elect can be deceived if they are not vigilant. This chapter explores the dangers of spiritual deception, how to recognize it, and the steps believers can take to guard against it.

The Reality of Spiritual Deception

Spiritual deception is a real and present danger in the life of every believer. The Bible makes it clear that the enemy, Satan, is a master of deceit. Jesus described him as "a liar and the father of lies" in John 8:44. From the very beginning, in the Garden of Eden, Satan used deception to lead humanity into sin, twisting God's words to create doubt and confusion (Gen. 3:1–5). This initial act of deception had catastrophic consequences, separating humanity from God and introducing sin into the world.

Throughout history, deception has remained one of Satan's primary tactics. He seeks to distort God's truth and lure people into believing lies that lead them away from their life-giving relationship with God. Deception can infiltrate any aspect of a believer's life. It can disrupt their understanding of Scripture and harm their relationships. It can cause them to make questionable moral decisions, even while believing they are "right." The deception of the enemy is not always blatant; often it is subtle and appears as "almost" truth, making it particularly dangerous.

The devil can deceive us in many ways, even in the church, from false teachings and beliefs to counterfeit spiritual experiences. He loves to cause division among God's people, making false accusations against men and women of God that other people choose to believe without proof. Believers are constantly bombarded with information from various sources, some of which may sound spiritually valid but is rooted in deception.

To guard against deception, it is crucial to recognize its signs and manifestations. Spiritual deception often begins subtly, making it all the more dangerous. Here are some common indicators:

- **Twisting Scripture**: One of the most common forms of deception is the twisting of Scripture to support false doctrines or beliefs. Beware if you hear someone taking verses out of context, adding to or subtracting from the Bible's teachings, or interpreting Scripture in ways that contradict the overall message of the gospel. Second Peter 3:16 warns that some people "distort [Paul's letters], as they do the other Scriptures, to their own destruction." Twisting Scripture is particularly insidious because something can appear to be true on the surface while subtly leading believers away from the true intent of God's Word.

- **Appealing to sensuality or worldly desires:** Deceptive teachings often appeal to our sinful nature, promising all of the blessings of God without the necessity of obeying Him. These teachings may downplay the need for repentance and godly living, focusing instead on material gain or personal success. Second Timothy 4:3–4 cautions, "For the time will come when people will not put up with sound doctrine. Instead, to suit their own desires, they will gather around them a great number of teachers to say what their itching ears want to hear. They will turn their ears away from the truth and turn aside to myths." These teachings can lead believers into a self-centered gospel that neglects the true message of Christ.

- **Focusing on self over God:** Deceptive teachings often place an excessive focus on self-glorification rather than on God's sovereignty and glory. This emphasis can lead believers away from the humility and submission that are essential to the Christian life. James 4:6 reminds us, "God opposes the proud but shows favor to the humble." A gospel that centers on self rather than on God is a perversion of the true gospel, leading to spiritual pride and a diminished reverence for God.

- **Isolating from godly counsel:**

  Isolation ➡ Temptation ➡ Spiritual Deprivation

  This simple progression illustrates a profound spiritual truth. When isolation takes root, it often leads to vulnerability, making it easier to fall into temptation. Over time, unchecked temptation results in spiritual deprivation—a state of distance from God's presence and purpose. Recognizing this cycle is the first step to breaking free and reclaiming the fullness of life God desires for us.

Deception often thrives in isolation. When individuals or groups isolate themselves from the broader body of Christ, they become more susceptible to adopting erroneous beliefs without the correction and balance that the community provides. Proverbs 18:1 warns, "A man who isolates himself seeks his own desire; he rages against all wise judgment" (NKJV). Isolation can create an echo chamber where only like-minded, potentially deceptive voices are heard, leading to deeper entrenchment in false beliefs about God, oneself, and others.

Developing Discernment

Discernment is the ability to genuinely distinguish between truth and error. If we cannot tell the difference between good and evil, it is easy to fall into sin! The Holy Spirit helps us discern what is real and what is counterfeit. This kind of discernment is a vital tool in guarding against spiritual deception. The Bible speaks of discernment as a gift of the Holy Spirit, given to believers to help them navigate the complexities of the spiritual realm (1 Cor. 12:10).

To cultivate discernment, we must develop a deep, intimate knowledge of God's Word. Hebrews 4:12 describes the Word of God as "alive and active. Sharper than any double-edged sword, it penetrates even to dividing soul and spirit, joints and marrow; it judges the thoughts and attitudes of the heart." The greatest thing you can do to develop spiritual discernment is to immerse yourself in Scripture. This practice will equip you to recognize when something doesn't align with God's truth. This deep engagement with the Bible enables you to identify deviations from biblical truth, even when such deviations are subtle or clothed in spiritual language.

Prayer is also essential for developing discernment. Asking the Holy Spirit for guidance and wisdom in all things helps believers stay sensitive to His leading and avoid being misled. James 1:5 encourages us to seek wisdom from God, promising that "if any of you lacks wisdom, you should ask God, who gives generously to all without finding fault, and it will be given to you." Regularly seeking God's guidance in prayer cultivates a sensitivity to His voice, making it easier to detect deception.

Finally, seeking counsel from mature and trusted believers can provide valuable perspective and confirmation when discerning whether something is from God or not. Proverbs 15:22 reminds us, "Plans fail for lack of counsel, but with many advisers they succeed." Engaging with a community of believers helps protect against isolation, where deception can more easily take root. A godly community provides checks and balances, helping individuals discern truth more accurately.

The Role of the Holy Spirit in Guarding Against Deception

The Holy Spirit plays a crucial role in protecting believers from deception. Jesus referred to the Holy Spirit as the "Spirit of truth," who would guide His followers into all truth (John 16:13). The Holy Spirit illuminates the Scriptures, brings understanding, and helps us apply God's Word to our lives accurately.

To rely on the Holy Spirit for guidance, we must cultivate a relationship with Him through prayer, worship, and obedience. The more attuned we are to the Holy Spirit's voice, the more easily we can recognize when something is not from God. Romans 8:14 tells us, "For those who are led by the Spirit of God are the children of God." Being led by the Spirit serves as a safeguard against deception, for the Holy Spirit will never contradict God's Word.

In addition to guiding believers into truth, the Holy Spirit also convicts us of sin and righteousness (John 16:8). This conviction is vital for guarding against deception, as it helps us stay on the right path and avoid falling into error. When we sense the Holy Spirit's conviction, it's important to respond quickly and repent if necessary, ensuring that our hearts remain aligned with God's will. Ignoring the Holy Spirit's conviction can result in spiritual dullness, making it easier to fall into deception.

This brings me to another role of the Holy Spirit—He empowers believers with discernment, enabling us to see beyond the surface and perceive the spiritual realities behind situations. This discernment is vital in a world filled with spiritual counterfeits. The Holy Spirit operates in our lives to help us discern the difference between truth and error, even when deception is cleverly disguised.

Discernment is key in spiritual warfare. As we lean on the Holy Spirit, He guides us in spiritual warfare, helping us recognize and resist the enemy's deceptive tactics. Ephesians 6:12 reminds us, "For our struggle is not against flesh and blood, but against the rulers, against the authorities, against the powers of this dark world and against the spiritual forces of evil in the heavenly realms." In this battle, the Holy Spirit equips believers with the necessary spiritual armor, including the belt of truth and the sword of the Spirit, which is the Word of God (Eph. 6:14–17). Have you put your armor on today?

The Holy Spirit also empowers us to live out the truth of the gospel each day. This empowerment is essential for us to overcome deception, as it allows us to understand the truth in our minds. Even more importantly, as we walk in the Spirit, we are empowered to live out the truth through our actions and decisions. Galatians 5:16 encourages, "So I say, walk by the Spirit, and you will not gratify the desires of the flesh." Walking by the Spirit keeps believers aligned with God's will and protects them from the deceptions that appeal to the flesh.

Finally, one of the most important aspects of the Holy Spirit's role is cultivating spiritual sensitivity in believers. This sensitivity allows us to detect even the slightest deviation from God's truth. By staying close to the Holy Spirit through regular prayer, worship, and obedience, we can develop a heightened awareness of His guidance and promptings, making us less likely to fall into deception.

Practical Steps to Guard Against Deception

Guarding against deception requires vigilance and a commitment to truth. Here are some steps believers can take:

Regularly study and meditate on Scripture. Knowing the Bible thoroughly is the first line of defense against deception. You should make it a regular habit to study and meditate on Scripture daily, allowing God's Word to shape your thoughts, which will then affect your actions. In John 17:17, Jesus said, "Sanctify them by the truth; your word is truth." The more familiar we are with the truth of God's Word, the more easily we can recognize when something is false.

Stay connected to a faithful community. Being part of a church community that faithfully teaches God's Word and encourages accountability is crucial. Fellow believers can offer support when we are going through challenges, praying for us and offering guidance as they can. They can also give correction when needed, helping to guard against deception. Hebrews 10:25 urges believers not to give up meeting together, "but encouraging one another—and all the more as you see the Day approaching." A strong community of faith provides a safety net, offering wisdom and perspective that can protect against being led astray. Don't succumb to the temptation of dividing from the church.

Pray for discernment and protection. Regularly pray for discernment and ask God to protect you from deception. Ephesians 6:18 encourages believers to "pray in the Spirit on all occasions with all kinds of prayers and requests." Asking God to guard your heart and mind is an important part of spiritual warfare. Prayer keeps us connected to God's truth and aligns our hearts with His will, making us less susceptible to the enemy's lies.

Avoid spiritual pride. Recognize that no one is immune to deception, and always remain humble before God. Spiritual pride can make believers more susceptible to deception, as it blinds them to their own weaknesses. First Corinthians 10:12 warns, "So, if you think you are standing firm, be careful that you don't fall!" Maintaining a humble and teachable spirit helps protect against deception. It's essential to remain open to correction and to recognize that growth in spiritual maturity includes a continuous need for God's guidance.

Examine the fruit. Jesus taught that we can recognize anything spiritually counterfeit by its fruits (Matt. 7:16). When you are evaluating certain ministries or spiritual movements, it's important to look at the long-term fruit they produce. Does it lead to greater love, joy, peace, patience, kindness, goodness, faithfulness, gentleness, and self-control (Gal. 5:22–23, ESV)? Or does it result in division, strife, and ungodliness? Examining the fruit helps us discern whether something is truly from God or is a deception.

Remain anchored in Christ. It's crucial to anchor yourself in the core doctrines of the Christian faith. Understanding the foundational truths of the gospel—such as the nature of God, the person and work of Jesus Christ, and the role of the Holy Spirit—provides a solid framework for discerning truth from error. Ephesians 4:14 warns against being "tossed back and forth by the waves, and blown here and there by every wind of teaching." By holding fast to sound doctrine, we can avoid being swayed by false teachings.

The Consequences of Falling into Deception

The consequences of falling into deception can be severe. And they don't just affect our relationship with God. They can be extremely detrimental to our relationships and our witness to others. Deception can lead to the following:

- **Spiritual stagnation or regression:** When believers embrace false beliefs or practices, they may find themselves drifting away from God's truth, leading to spiritual stagnation or even regression in their faith. As a result, their relationship with God may weaken. Their spiritual vitality may diminish, and their ability to hear God's voice may fade.

- **Broken relationships:** Deception can cause divisions within all sorts of relationships, particularly when false beliefs or practices create conflicts. The enemy uses deception to sow discord among believers, undermining unity and causing strife. Ephesians 4:3 urges us to "make every effort to keep the unity of the Spirit through the bond of peace." However, when deception takes root, it can erode this unity, leading to broken relationships and a fractured community.

- **Loss of witness:** Believers who fall into deception may lose credibility in their witness to others, leading people away from the truth of the gospel instead of toward it. This can have eternal consequences, as those who are misled may never come to know the true saving power of Jesus Christ. In Matthew 5:13, Jesus warned, "You are the salt of the earth. But if the salt loses its saltiness, how can it be made salty again? It is no longer good for anything, except to be thrown out and trampled underfoot." Maintaining a pure and truthful witness is essential for fulfilling the Great Commission.

- **Opening of demonic portals:** As we have discussed in previous chapters, embracing deception can open demonic portals, inviting spiritual oppression and bondage into your life. These portals can manifest in various ways, such as increased anxiety and a sense of spiritual heaviness. When believers stray from God's truth, they can inadvertently give the enemy a foothold in their lives, leading to increased spiritual warfare and a diminished sense of God's presence.

- **Stunted spiritual growth:** Deception stunts spiritual growth by leading believers down paths that focus on secondary issues or distractions that don't produce anything worthwhile, preventing them from maturing in their faith and experiencing the fullness of life that God intends for them. Hebrews 5:12–14 speaks of the importance of moving beyond elementary teachings and growing in discernment so that we can "distinguish good from evil."

Guarding against deception is a critical aspect of the Christian life. By staying grounded in God's Word, relying on the Holy Spirit, and practicing discernment, we can protect ourselves from the enemy's lies and remain steadfast in the truth. Deception is a subtle and dangerous trap, but with vigilance and a commitment to truth, it can be avoided.

As you continue your spiritual journey, remember that God has equipped you with everything you need to walk in truth and guard against the enemy's schemes. Cultivate a deep relationship with God as you spend time with Him throughout your day, and surround yourself with a community of believers who are committed to upholding the truth. By doing so, you will protect yourself and those around you from deception. May you walk in the light of God's truth, free from deception and fully empowered to fulfill the calling He has placed on your life!

Spiritual deception is one of the most dangerous and subtle tools the enemy uses to derail believers from the path of truth. It can creep into our lives in various forms. We can go through misleading experiences, or others can mischaracterize or even condemn their brothers and sisters in Christ. We may even be drawn away from God through the influence of our own desires. The stakes are high, as falling into deception can lead to broken relationships and even the opening of demonic portals that bring oppression and bondage.

However, God has not left us defenseless. He has equipped us with His Word, the guidance of the Holy Spirit, and the support of a community of believers to guard against deception. By staying deeply rooted in Scripture, cultivating a close relationship with the Holy Spirit, and practicing discernment, we can navigate the complexities of the spiritual realm and stand firm in the truth.

As you move forward in your spiritual journey, commit to regularly seeking God's wisdom and protection. Engage with His Word daily, surround yourself with trustworthy believers who will encourage and challenge you, and always be mindful of the enemy's tactics. Remember that humility and a teachable spirit are your greatest allies in staying aligned with God's truth.

In a world filled with voices vying for your attention, choose to listen to the voice of truth. May your life be a beacon of light, shining brightly in a world that desperately needs the clarity and hope that only the gospel can provide. As you guard against deception and walk in truth, you will protect your own spiritual well-being. In addition, you will become a source of strength and guidance for others who are seeking to navigate the same path.

May the Lord bless you with the wisdom and discernment you need to follow Him faithfully and the unwavering resolve to stand firm in His truth, now and always.

Activation Prayer

Heavenly Father, I come before You with a humble heart, acknowledging my need for Your truth and guidance. Lord, I thank You for equipping me with Your Word and the Holy Spirit to guard against deception. Help me stay vigilant and anchored in Your truth, even in a world filled with lies and distractions.

Father, I pray for those who may have fallen into deception. Reveal Your truth to them. Break every chain of falsehood, and open their eyes to see Your light. Restore them to Your path and purpose, and use me as a vessel of Your love and truth in their lives.

Guard my heart, Lord, from pride and the schemes of the enemy. Keep me humble, teachable, and aligned with Your will. Strengthen my commitment to Your Word and to the community of believers You have placed around me.

Thank You for being the Spirit of truth, who leads me into all understanding. I place my trust in You, knowing that You are faithful to guide and protect me. In the mighty name of Jesus, I pray. Amen.

DID YOU KNOW?

The brain's prefrontal cortex is responsible for critical thinking and discernment. Regular engagement with Scripture strengthens this area, helping believers guard against deception by discerning truth from falsehood.

PORTALS IN POP CULTURE:
The Upside Down in *Stranger Things* (2016–Present TV series)

The Netflix series *Stranger Things* introduced audiences to the "Upside Down," a dark, alternate dimension that parallels the real world but is filled with sinister entities. The series highlights the consequences of scientific experiments (like those at Hawkins Lab) that unintentionally open portals, unleashing evil into the natural world. As this book explores, we are called to open the gates of heaven, not peer into the shadows. Be vigilant. The enemy uses images, visuals, and storylines like these to stir a curiosity toward darkness. Don't be distracted or drawn in. Stay anchored in truth, and guard your spirit from the subtle pull of deception.

CHAPTER 14

ENGAGING IN SPIRITUAL WARFARE

SOME TIME AGO my prayer team, a group of devoted intercessors, approached me with heavy hearts. This group had been instrumental in the ministry, initially fervent in their faith and consistent in their prayer gatherings. But something had shifted.

They were now facing intense spiritual attacks, feeling weary and drained, both spiritually and physically.

They came to me, discouraged, seeking direction. Some even suggested pausing the prayer meetings altogether, feeling as though their efforts were under relentless assault. As I listened, I could sense the weight of their struggles, but I also discerned that this was not a time to retreat.

I entered a time of prayer, seeking God's guidance for this vital ministry. During that time, the Holy Spirit began to stir within me a message of encouragement and truth. I returned to the team with a renewed sense of urgency and purpose.

I shared with them what the Holy Spirit had revealed: The reason for the heightened attacks on the prayer ministry was that this was the area God intended to use most powerfully in that season. The enemy, knowing this, sought to disrupt their efforts, sending arrows of discouragement and disconnection to stop them from advancing.

With this revelation, I admonished and encouraged them with this insight, urging them not to give in to the enemy's schemes but to stand firm in their calling. Strengthened by the word of the Lord, the team returned to their prayer meetings with renewed fervor.

What followed was nothing short of miraculous. Where there had been a sense of heaviness and disconnect, now there was a fresh wind of the Spirit. The fire of God reignited their hearts, and a supernatural atmosphere began to manifest in their gatherings. The meetings were transformed, and the team experienced a new-found sensitivity to the Holy Spirit.

As the prayer team persisted, the impact spread. Those who had previously shown little interest in prayer gatherings began inquiring about the meetings, and new members joined the team. The ministry once again began to flourish, growing in numbers and spiritual strength. This renewal was a direct result of the team's commitment to engage in spiritual warfare and intercession despite the attacks they faced.

This experience serves as a testament to the power of perseverance in spiritual warfare. When we remain faithful and continue to seek God, even in the face of opposition, His power breaks through, bringing victory and transformation.

Spiritual warfare is an integral part of the Christian life, a battle that every believer must engage in as we seek to advance God's kingdom and resist the forces of darkness. Understanding the nature of this battle, the weapons available to us, and the strategies needed to be victorious is crucial for maintaining spiritual authority and keeping heavenly portals open.

The Reality of Spiritual Warfare

The conflict between the kingdom of God and the kingdom of darkness is ongoing, and it influences every aspect of our lives. The apostle Paul emphasized this in Ephesians 6:12: "For our struggle is not against flesh and blood, but against the rulers, against the authorities, against the powers of this dark world and against the spiritual forces of evil in the heavenly realms."

This battle is pervasive, affecting every area of our lives. The struggle can take place in our thoughts and emotions, affecting our relationships and even our circumstances. It is not confined to a specific time or place. From the moment we accept Christ, we are enlisted in this spiritual conflict. Yet God, in His grace, has not left us unprepared. He has equipped us with spiritual weapons and armor, empowering us to stand firm against the enemy's schemes and advance His kingdom.

Sometimes people think that spiritual warfare is something only "spiritual" people in ministry have to take on, but that is not the case. *Every* believer is called to engage in this battle. Our lives become a battleground where the forces of light and darkness contend for influence, and our response to this reality determines the outcome.

Now let's go deeper into an aspect of warfare with which many are not familiar. Mysteries are being revealed to you for God's glory!

Warfare in the Air
(the Arena of Our Thoughts)

> And you He made alive, who were dead in trespasses and sins, in which you once walked according to the course of this world, according to the prince of the power of the air, the spirit who now works in the sons of disobedience.
> —Ephesians 2:1–2, nkjv

Have you ever felt like there's a battle raging in your mind—a constant pull between truth and lies, peace and chaos, faith and fear? You're not imagining it. The Bible makes it clear that there's a very real spiritual battle happening, and much of it takes place in what the apostle Paul describes as the "air." In Ephesians 2:1–2, Paul revealed that before we were made alive in Christ, we were influenced by "the prince of the power of the air" (nkjv), referring to Satan, who operates in the unseen realms of thought and atmosphere.

This battle is not just an abstract concept. Paul connects it to our daily lives again in Ephesians 6:12, reminding us that our struggle isn't against flesh and blood but against spiritual forces in the heavenly realms. When you put these two passages together, you begin to see a picture of warfare that takes place in the air—both in the spiritual atmosphere around us and in the battlefield of the mind within us.

The "air" represents the realm where spiritual influences—both godly and demonic—intersect with human thought, decisions, and emotions. The enemy targets this realm to sow confusion, fear, doubt, and temptation. He knows that if he can influence the way we think, he can impact the way we live. The mind becomes the gateway through which the battle for our peace and our purpose is fought.

The good news is that we are *not* powerless in this battle! If the enemy operates in the air, we counter in the air—with prayer, the Word of God, and the renewing of our minds. Paul reminds us in 2 Corinthians 10:5 to take "every thought into captivity to the obedience of Christ" (NKJV). This is where the battle begins—by intentionally aligning our thoughts with God's truth and refusing to let the enemy take up residence in our minds.

Every time you pray, declare God's promises, or worship, you're filling the atmosphere with heaven's truth and power. You aren't being reactionary to what the enemy is sending your way. You're proactively shifting the environment and taking authority over the air. Prayer is a formidable spiritual weapon! When you pray, you're stepping into the spiritual realm with the authority of Christ to silence the enemy and establish God's truth.

Ephesians 6:11 also reminds us to put on the full armor of God. The helmet of salvation guards our minds from the lies and accusations of the enemy, while the sword of the Spirit—the Word of God—equips us to strike down deception and declare victory.

If we're going to win this battle, we have to recognize that much of it takes place in the mind. The enemy works tirelessly to flood the air with lies and distractions because he knows that our thoughts shape our lives. But he doesn't have the final say. Jesus has already secured the victory, and through Him, we have the power to stand firm and overcome.

This isn't a passive fight. It's a daily choice to renew your mind, to counter lies with truth, and to fill your heart and home with

God's Word and presence. The enemy may try to claim the air, but the air belongs to God—and so do you.

As we explore this topic of spiritual warfare together, I want to encourage you: You're not alone in this fight. You have the tools, the authority, and the power to reclaim the air, both in your mind and in your atmosphere. The battle may be fierce, but the victory is secure. Jesus has already won, and because of Him, you can stand strong.

The concept of air in the Bible holds profound symbolic and spiritual meanings. Air represents life and spirit. Think of the air in your lungs that brings life to your body. It also signifies power and dominion in the spiritual realm. Its significance spans both the Old and New Testaments, with the Hebrew and Greek terms shedding light on its depth.

The Biblical Symbolism of Air

Old Testament: Hebrew (חוּר, ruach)

Primary meaning: *Ruach* translates to "spirit," "breath," or "wind." While it can mean "air," it primarily represents the invisible force sustaining life and the presence of God.

Significance: Genesis 2:7 reveals, "Then the LORD God formed a man from the dust of the ground and breathed into his nostrils the breath (*ruach*) of life, and man became a living being." Here, air symbolizes life and vitality directly from God.

Symbolic insight: In passages like Ezekiel 37:5–10, *ruach* breathes life into dry bones, symbolizing God's power to renew and restore.

New Testament: Greek (πνεῦμα, pneuma)

Primary meaning: *Pneuma* shares similarities with *ruach*, meaning "spirit," "breath," or "air." It signifies the Holy Spirit, life, and spiritual presence.

Significance: Jesus equates *pneuma* with the unseen yet transformative power of the Spirit, as seen in John 3:8: "The wind (*pneuma*) blows where it wishes.…So is everyone who is born of the Spirit (*pneuma*)" (NKJV).

Symbolic insight: Acts 2:2–4 vividly depicts the Holy Spirit's arrival as "a rushing mighty wind" (NKJV), emphasizing God's empowering presence through air.

Symbolic Themes of Air

- **Air as life and spirit:** Air embodies God's breath and Spirit, essential for sustaining all life.

- **Air as the Holy Spirit:** It symbolizes the Spirit's empowering, unseen, and transformative role in believers' lives.

- **Air as the unseen realm:** Representing spiritual influence, air highlights both God's sovereignty and the enemy's opposition.

- **Air as hope of eternity:** The promise of meeting Christ in the air signifies eternal communion and salvation.

In both physical and spiritual warfare, establishing "air superiority" is crucial. In military strategy, air superiority disrupts communication and secures dominance before ground operations begin. Spiritually, prayer serves this function:

- **Prayer disrupts enemy communication:** It dismantles the schemes of the adversary and establishes divine authority in the spiritual realm.

- **Prayer establishes superiority:** Just as aerial campaigns cripple enemy infrastructure, prayer builds a spiritual stronghold, enabling believers to stand firm.

As Paul wrote in 2 Corinthians 2:11, "Lest Satan should take advantage of us; for we are not ignorant of his devices" (NKJV). To remain vigilant, we have to arm ourselves with the truth about our enemy and then actively fight against him.

Practical Insights into Spiritual Warfare

Spiritual warfare is a reality for every believer, each and every day. Paul reminds us in Ephesians 6:12 that our struggle is not against flesh and blood but against spiritual forces. This constant battle requires (1) awareness, recognizing that life is a battleground for influence; (2) preparation, employing God's armor and spiritual weapons to resist the enemy's schemes; and (3) action, consistent prayer and alignment with God's Word to secure victory.

Without proper defenses, believers become vulnerable to spiritual attacks, making them *WEAK*:

Wavering: characterized by indecision or lack of conviction

Exhausted: depleted of spiritual strength

Aimless: operating without purpose or direction

Knowledge-lacking: Missing the wisdom to discern and counteract enemy strategies

Ultimately, the battle is the Lord's. By aligning ourselves with God's Spirit and engaging in prayer, we establish dominion in the unseen realms, securing victory through His power. As Jesus assured in John 8:36, "If the Son makes you free, you shall be free indeed" (NKJV). The believer's freedom and empowerment come through a renewed mind, a fortified spirit, and unwavering trust in the God who reigns supreme.

Understanding the Armor of God

The armor of God, described in Ephesians 6:13–18, is the divine provision that enables believers to withstand the enemy's attacks and remain standing in victory. Each piece of the armor has a specific purpose, and together they form a comprehensive defense system that also empowers us to take the offensive in spiritual warfare.

- **The belt of truth:** The belt of truth is foundational because truth holds everything together. In a world filled with deception, grounding ourselves in God's truth is critical. Jesus said, "Then you will know the truth, and the truth will set you free" (John 8:32). By living honestly and embracing God's Word as the ultimate truth, we protect ourselves from the enemy's lies and distortions.

- **The breastplate of righteousness:** The breastplate covers and protects the heart, representing the righteousness of Christ, which shields us from the enemy's accusations. This righteousness is not our own but is imputed to us through faith in Jesus. It serves as a defense against the attacks of guilt and condemnation. As 2 Corinthians 5:21 reminds us, "God made him who had no sin to be sin for us, so that in him we might become the righteousness of God."

- **The shoes of the gospel of peace:** The shoes equip us to stand firm and move forward in our mission to spread the gospel. The peace of God stabilizes us, allowing us to remain unshaken by external circumstances. Isaiah 52:7 beautifully captures this: "How beautiful on the mountains are the feet of those who bring good news, who proclaim peace, who bring good tidings, who proclaim salvation."

- **The shield of faith:** Faith is a defensive weapon that extinguishes the fiery darts of fear and deception that the enemy hurls at us. Hebrews 11:1 defines *faith* as "confidence in what we hope for and assurance about what we do not see." Holding up the shield of faith means trusting in God's promises and His faithfulness, even when circumstances seem bleak.

- **The helmet of salvation:** The helmet protects our minds, symbolizing the assurance of our salvation and the renewal of our thoughts in Christ. The enemy often targets the mind with doubts and fears, but the helmet of salvation guards our thoughts and reminds us of our secure identity in Christ. Philippians 2:5 states, "Let this mind be in you which was also in Christ Jesus" (NKJV).

- **The sword of the Spirit:** The sword, representing the Word of God, is both an offensive and a defensive weapon. Hebrews 4:12 describes it as "alive and active" and "sharper than any double-edged sword." By declaring and applying Scripture, we cut through the lies of the enemy and advance God's kingdom.

Strategies for Engaging in Spiritual Warfare

To be effective in spiritual warfare, believers must adopt strategies that align with God's Word and the leading of the Holy Spirit. These strategies involve both defensive and offensive actions, ensuring protection while proactively advancing God's kingdom.

- **Know your enemy:** Understanding the enemy's nature and tactics is crucial. The Bible describes Satan as a deceiver, accuser, and tempter whose primary goal is to "steal and kill and destroy" (John 10:10). Recognizing his methods, such as lies, temptation, and fear, allows us to counter them effectively with God's truth and power.

- **Stand firm in faith:** Spiritual warfare requires an unshakable faith in God's promises and a steadfast commitment to His will. James 4:7 advises, "Submit yourselves, then, to God. Resist the devil, and he will flee from you." Standing firm means refusing to be swayed by the enemy's lies or intimidation and holding fast to the truth of God's Word.

- **Use the Word of God:** The Word of God is our primary weapon in spiritual warfare. Jesus demonstrated its power when He countered Satan's temptations in the wilderness by declaring, "It is written" (Matt. 4:4, 7, 10). By knowing and speaking Scripture, we resist the enemy and assert God's authority in our lives.

- **Maintain a life of prayer:** Prayer is both our line of communication with God and a powerful weapon in warfare. When we pray, He answers! He gives us the guidance and strength we need to win the victory, and He protects us from the enemy's plans. And when we intercede for others, we break the power of the enemy in their lives. First Thessalonians 5:17 simply states, "Pray continually," highlighting the importance of constant communion with God.

- **Live in holiness and obedience:** Holiness and obedience to God's commands are critical defenses against the enemy. Sin creates openings for the enemy to gain a foothold in our lives, while obedience closes those doors. First Peter 1:15–16 calls us to live holy lives because God is holy. By aligning our lives with God's will, we fortify our position in spiritual warfare.

- **Stay connected to the body of Christ:** Spiritual warfare is not meant to be fought in isolation. Ecclesiastes 4:12 reminds us, "Though one may be overpowered, two can defend themselves. A cord of three strands is not quickly broken." Staying connected to a community of believers strengthens us and provides additional resources in the battle.

Praise and worship are additional powerful tools in spiritual warfare that shift our focus from our circumstances to God's greatness. When we worship, we invite God's presence into our situations, which disarms the enemy and confuses his plans.

Worship opens the heavenly portals and allows God's intervention to come into our lives, right where we need it the most. Psalm 149:6–9 speaks of the power of praise in warfare: "May the praise of God be in their mouths and a double-edged sword in their hands" (v. 6). When we engage in worship, we align ourselves with God's power and authority, overcoming the enemy through the joy and victory that come from God.

Overcoming Fear in Spiritual Warfare

Fear is one of the enemy's most potent weapons in spiritual warfare. It can paralyze believers, causing them to hesitate or withdraw from the battle. However, the Bible repeatedly tells us not to fear. Second Timothy 1:7 declares, "For the Spirit God gave us does not make us timid, but gives us power, love and self-discipline."

To overcome fear, we must focus on God's truth rather than the enemy's lies. Meditating on scriptures that speak of God's protection and faithfulness can help dispel fear and build confidence. Psalm 27:1 is a powerful reminder: "The LORD is my light and my salvation—whom shall I fear? The LORD is the stronghold of my life—of whom shall I be afraid?"

Recalling past victories and God's faithfulness also helps combat fear. When we remember how God has delivered us before, our faith is strengthened, and we are reassured of His ability to do so again.

Spiritual warfare is an inevitable aspect of the Christian life, requiring believers to be vigilant, equipped, and ready to engage the enemy at all times. Understanding the reality of this battle, putting on the full armor of God, and employing the spiritual weapons He has provided—such as prayer, the Word of God, and praise—are essential for standing firm against the enemy's schemes and securing victory in our spiritual lives.

As you continue to walk in faith, remember that the battle ultimately belongs to the Lord. He has already secured the ultimate victory through Jesus Christ, and you fight from a position of triumph. The challenges and conflicts you face are opportunities to grow in your dependence on God, to strengthen your spiritual muscles, and to experience His power in new ways.

Engage in spiritual warfare with confidence, knowing that you are not alone. The entire body of Christ, both on earth and in heaven, stands with you in this battle. You are surrounded by a great cloud of witnesses who have fought the good fight and have entered into their reward (Heb. 12:1). Their testimony, along with the promises of God, should inspire and encourage you to persevere, even when the battle is fierce.

In your personal life, but also in the greater community where you live and minister, you are called to be a beacon of light, driving back the darkness and opening portals for God's kingdom to advance. Every action you take in alignment with God's will has a profound impact in the spiritual realm.

As you move forward, remember to put on the armor of God daily. Stay close to the Lord, and He will help you discern when you are facing an attack by the enemy, especially when you are relying on the power of the Holy Spirit. His plan for you is not just to secure your own spiritual victory, but He wants to send you out to contribute to the advancement of His kingdom on the earth. The enemy's strongholds will crumble, and you will witness the transformative power of God at work in your life and in the world around you. I can't think of anything better than that!

May you walk in the authority that Christ has given you— with courage and conviction—knowing that you are more than a conqueror through Him who loves you (Rom. 8:37). And may you see the enemy's strongholds fall as you advance God's kingdom in every area of your life.

Activation Prayer

Heavenly Father, I come before You in humility and faith, acknowledging the reality of the spiritual battles we face. Thank You for equipping me with Your armor and for the power of Your Word, which enables me to stand firm against the enemy's schemes.

Lord, I ask for Your strength and guidance as I engage in spiritual warfare. Help me to remain steadfast, to persevere in prayer and intercession, and to trust in Your promises. When I face discouragement and weariness, remind me of Your faithfulness, and renew my spirit with Your presence.

I pray for every believer who is fighting battles in the spiritual realm. Cover them with Your protection. Fill them with Your peace, and surround them with a community of support and encouragement. May Your light shine brightly through each of us, driving back the darkness and advancing the light of Your kingdom on earth.

Lord, I declare victory in the name of Jesus. I thank You for all the amazing plans You have for me, for all the strongholds that are being torn down, and for the lives that are being transformed by Your power. To You be all the glory, honor, and praise. In Jesus' mighty name, we pray. Amen.

DID YOU KNOW?

In high-stress situations, the brain's fight-or-flight response can overshadow rational thinking. Prayer and worship counteract this response by activating the parasympathetic nervous system, calming the mind and empowering believers to focus on spiritual strategies.

PORTALS IN POP CULTURE:
Haunted Locations and Demonic Portals

Notable locations like the Stanley Hotel in Colorado (inspiration for Stephen King's *The Shining*) and the Cecil Hotel in Los Angeles are rumored to be sites of intense spiritual activity, often tied to demonic portals. Paranormal investigators frequently report chilling phenomena in these places, including apparitions, unexplained sounds, and oppressive feelings. While these locations fascinate many, they also serve as a warning: Not all curiosity is harmless. Some atmospheres are charged with darkness and designed to bait the soul into spiritual vulnerability. As I reveal in this book, we are opening either gates to heaven or gateways to hell. Avoid such spaces. Don't play with the demonic or entertain what God has called you to resist. Remain anchored in Christ, covered in His truth, and guarded in His presence so that no door is opened that invites darkness in.

CHAPTER 15

LIVING IN THE VICTORY OF HEAVENLY PORTALS

VIVIDLY RECALL A moment when I faced an unexpected and intense spiritual attack—an assault that sought to disrupt my life and ministry. I had fallen gravely ill, struck by a sudden and inexplicable sickness that left me bewildered. The medic who checked me out could only observe the symptoms on the surface; they could not determine the root cause.

I knew immediately that this was no ordinary sickness; it was a spiritual battle. Confined to my bed for nearly two weeks, I grew physically weak, was unable to eat, and rapidly lost weight. My muscles ached, chills strained my body, and fever consumed me. One night, as I lay overwhelmed by pain and fatigue, something extraordinary occurred.

A cold breeze swept into my bedroom, carrying with it an oppressive and dark presence. I immediately discerned that this was not an angelic visitation. The atmosphere in my room had turned ominous. Unable to move my body, I sensed something close to me, mocking me and laughing in a sinister tone. I could feel its breath and hear its laughter; then its oppressive words filled the room.

I asked, "Who are you?" The response came, chilling and direct: "We have done this to you." The spirit revealed its intention—to kill me. It was then that I realized this attack was an attempt to derail all the mighty victories God had been accomplishing in my life and ministry.

Though my body was immobilized, my spirit was stirred to fight. I began to call on the name of the Lord with all the strength I could muster. With a deep spiritual determination, I declared, "You are a liar! I already have the victory!"

As soon as I proclaimed these words, the oppressive presence fled. The cold chills in my body dissipated, and a profound peace entered my room. It was after that night that my physical strength returned. My health was restored because the spiritual fight had been won through the name of the Lord Jesus. That experience strengthened my resolve even more to wage war against the powers of darkness that sought to steal, kill, and destroy!

This experience, instead of deterring me, became a catalyst for deeper determination. It reignited my passion to press forward in God's work, knowing that the attacks of the enemy were proof of the kingdom impact being made. That moment taught me that victory is not something we hope for—it is a reality we walk in, secured by the power of Christ.

As believers, we are called to live in the victory that Christ has already secured for us—a present reality that we can experience daily. By engaging with heavenly portals and walking in the power of God's kingdom, we can live in the fullness of this victory. This final chapter explores how to maintain this victory in the face of challenges, how to ensure the continual flow of God's blessings through heavenly portals, and how to share this victorious life with others.

Understanding Our Victory in Christ

The foundation of our victory as believers is rooted in the finished work of Jesus Christ. Through His death and resurrection, Jesus decisively defeated sin, death, and the powers of darkness. This truth has eternal implications for us and for the devil and his minions! Colossians 2:15 declares, "And having disarmed the powers and authorities, he made a public spectacle of them, triumphing over them by the cross." This is the essence of our victory—Christ's triumph is complete, and it is a victory in which we are invited to share.

Living in victory means recognizing that we are no longer bound by the chains of sin, fear, or the enemy's schemes. Romans 8:37

reminds us, "No, in all these things we are more than conquerors through him who loved us." The phrase "more than conquerors" suggests that our victory in Christ goes beyond mere survival; it implies a state of overwhelming triumph, a life lived in the abundance that Jesus promised in John 10:10: "The thief comes only to steal and kill and destroy; I have come that they may have life, and have it to the full."

This victory is comprehensive, covering every aspect of our lives. Jesus secured complete and total victory over every power that stands against the kingdom of God. When we embrace this truth, we can begin to live with the confidence and authority that come from knowing that we are on the winning side.

To live in continuous victory, it is essential to keep heavenly portals open in our lives, allowing God's power and blessings to flow freely. This kind of life involves maintaining a strong connection with God and consistently applying the spiritual principles we have learned throughout our journey of faith, including the following.

Spend time with God daily. Regular prayer, worship, and Bible study are vital for maintaining an open portal to heaven. These practices keep us rooted in God's truth, sensitive to His voice, and filled with His Spirit. By prioritizing our relationship with God, we ensure that His victory continually manifests in our lives. Psalm 1:2–3 describes the person who delights in God's Word as being "like a tree planted by streams of water, which yields its fruit in season and whose leaf does not wither—whatever they do prospers." This imagery highlights the importance of being continually nourished by God's presence through daily communion.

Walk in obedience. Victory is closely tied to obedience. When we live according to God's commands, we align ourselves with His will and position ourselves to receive His blessings. Deuteronomy 28:1–2 promises that if we fully obey the Lord and carefully follow His commands, His blessings will overtake us. Obedience to God doesn't mean you follow the rules and that's it. It is about living in harmony with God's design for our lives. When we walk in obedience, we keep the heavenly portal open, allowing God's victory to flow uninterrupted.

Declare God's Word. Our words have power, and when we speak God's Word over our lives, we activate His promises and reinforce our victory. Proverbs 18:21 tells us that "the tongue has the power of life and death." By declaring God's truth, we resist the enemy's lies and affirm our identity as victors in Christ. This affirmation is more than just "positive thinking," as some people try to say. It is aligning the words of our mouths with the reality of God's kingdom and the authority of His Word, even in our everyday conversations. When we declare Scripture, we wield the sword of the Spirit, cutting through the lies and deceptions of the enemy. Watch what you say!

Standing firm in faith. Faith is the key to living in victory. Hebrews 11:1 defines *faith* as "confidence in what we hope for and assurance about what we do not see." Even when circumstances are challenging, faith allows us to stand firm, knowing that God's victory is already secured. James 1:6 encourages us to ask in faith without doubting, as doubt can hinder our ability to receive from God. Faith is not a passive belief but an active trust in God's promises, even in the face of adversity. It is the conviction that God is who He says He is and that He will do what He has promised.

Overcoming Challenges to Victory

While we are called to live in victory, we will inevitably face challenges that seek to undermine our faith and steal our joy. These challenges can come in various forms—temptations or personal struggles that are out of our control. However, by relying on God's strength and the tools He has given us, we can overcome these challenges and maintain our victory.

Resist the enemy. The enemy will attempt to steal our victory by attacking us with fear, doubt, and temptation. James 4:7 instructs us to "submit yourselves, then, to God. Resist the devil, and he will flee from you." By submitting to God and actively resisting the enemy, we can stand firm and maintain our victory. Resistance involves not only saying no to the enemy but also saying yes to God. It takes a conscious choice to align our thoughts and actions, even our attitudes, with God's truth rather than the enemy's lies.

Persevere through trials. Trials and difficulties are a natural part of life, but they do not have to rob us of our victory. Romans 5:3–4 encourages us to rejoice in our sufferings because suffering produces perseverance, character, and hope. Perseverance in the face of trials strengthens our faith and deepens our reliance on God, leading to greater victory. All of the challenges we are up against from day to day help us grow stronger in the Lord. When we face difficulties with a mindset of victory, we can emerge more resilient, fully equipped to handle whatever comes our way.

Rely on the Holy Spirit. The Holy Spirit is our Helper and Guide, empowering us to live victoriously. When we face challenges, we can rely on the Holy Spirit to give us wisdom, strength, and direction. Galatians 5:16 advises, "So I say, walk by the Spirit, and you will not gratify the desires of the flesh." Walking in the Spirit keeps us aligned with God's will and ensures that we continue to experience His victory. When we are in tune with the Spirit, we can navigate life's challenges with confidence, knowing that we are not alone.

Sharing the Victory with Others

When God moves in our lives, it's such a wonderful thing! But even better is the fact that living in victory gives us the amazing opportunity to share the goodness of God with others. As we experience God's victory in our lives, we are called to be witnesses of His power and help others step into the victory that is available through Christ.

One of the most powerful ways to share the victory is to testify of what God has done in our lives. Revelation 12:11 says, "They triumphed over him by the blood of the Lamb and by the word of their testimony." Our testimonies build up the faith of other people, pointing them to the source of true victory. Sharing our stories of God's faithfulness not only glorifies Him, but it also inspires others to trust in His power and provision.

As we walk in victory, we are called to encourage and disciple others who are struggling or seeking to grow in their faith. By coming alongside them, offering support, and sharing what we have learned, we help them experience the victory that Christ offers. First Thessalonians 5:11 encourages us to "encourage one another and build each other up." Discipleship is a hands-on deal! It involves walking with other people through daily life, showing them how to live in the victory that is theirs in Christ.

Victory in Christ also empowers us to serve and love others self-lessly. When we operate from a place of victory, we are free to give generously and love unconditionally. Galatians 5:13 reminds us, "You, my brothers and sisters, were called to be free. But do not use your freedom to indulge the flesh; rather, serve one another humbly in love." Serving others is a powerful way to demonstrate the victory of God's kingdom. When we freely receive God's grace, it only makes sense to pour it out to other people!

Another way to share the victory with others is through mentoring and leadership. By assuming roles of spiritual leadership—whether in the church, in small groups, or in informal settings—we can help guide others toward living in victory. Leadership is about influence more than it is about authority. When we mentor others, we pass on the wisdom and experience that have helped us live victoriously. Paul's relationship with Timothy is a prime example of this. Paul taught Timothy, certainly, but more importantly, he lived out his faith in front of him and encouraged Timothy to do the same. In 2 Timothy 2:2, Paul instructed Timothy, "And the things you have heard me say in the presence of many witnesses entrust to reliable people who will also be qualified to teach others." This verse underscores the importance of passing on the victory to the next generation of believers.

Living in victory also equips us to engage in evangelism and outreach more effectively. When others see the peace and joy that come from living in victory, they are often drawn to the source of that victory—Jesus Christ. First Peter 3:15 encourages believers always to be ready to answer everyone who asks about the hope we have. Sharing the gospel with others becomes a natural outflow of the victory we experience in our own lives. Our testimony of victory can serve as a powerful tool in evangelism, demonstrating that the Christian life is not following a list of religious do's and don'ts. It's about a real, transformative relationship with Jesus Christ.

Intercessory prayer is another crucial way to share victory with others. As we experience victory in our own lives, we can stand in the gap for others, praying that they, too, will experience God's victory. James 5:16 reminds us that "the prayer of a righteous person is powerful and effective." Praying for others is an act of love and faith, as we believe that God will bring them through their challenges and into the victory that He has promised.

Living in victory also means keeping our eyes fixed on the ultimate victory that is to come—the return of Christ and the establishment of His eternal kingdom. While we experience victory in this life, we also live in the hope of the final victory, when all things will be made new and every enemy will be defeated.

The return of Christ is the culmination of our victory. It is the moment when all of God's promises will be fulfilled and we will see the fullness of His kingdom established. Revelation 21:4–5 paints a beautiful picture of this future victory: "He will wipe every tear from their eyes. There will be no more death or mourning or crying or pain, for the old order of things has passed away. He who was seated on the throne said, 'I am making everything new!'" This promise gives us hope and strengthens our resolve to live victoriously now, knowing that our present struggles are temporary and that a glorious future awaits.

Living in the expectation of future victory means adopting an eternal perspective. It means recognizing that our lives on earth are just a small part of God's greater plan. This perspective helps us prioritize what truly matters—our relationship with God and our love for others. Colossians 3:2 advises us to "set your minds on things above, not on earthly things." When we live with eternity in mind, we are better able to navigate the challenges of life, knowing that our ultimate victory is secure.

The expectation of future victory also encourages us to persevere in our faith. Hebrews 10:36 says, "You need to persevere so that when you have done the will of God, you will receive what he has promised." Perseverance is key to living in victory. It is the determination to keep pressing forward, even when the journey is difficult, knowing that the final victory is worth the struggle. This perseverance is fueled by the hope of what is to come—the day when we will stand before God, fully redeemed and fully victorious.

While we look forward to the ultimate victory, it is also important to celebrate the small victories along the way. Each step of progress, each answered prayer, and each moment of victory are a testament to God's faithfulness. These small victories remind us that God is with us, that He is working in our lives, and that He is leading us toward the final victory. Psalm 126:3 says, "The LORD has done great things for us, and we are filled with joy." Celebrating small victories keeps us encouraged and motivated to continue walking in faith.

Living in victory allows us to leave a legacy for future generations as well. The choices we make, the faith we live out, and the victories we achieve can have a lasting impact on those who come after us. Deuteronomy 6:6–7 encourages us to pass on our faith to our children, teaching them to love and obey God. By living in victory and teaching others to do the same, we build a legacy that honors God and advances His kingdom.

Living in victory is the culmination of everything we have explored throughout this book. It is the daily experience of God's presence as we walk in the authority and freedom that Christ has secured for us. This victory is not just a concept, but it is a reality that we can live in every day, regardless of the challenges we face.

As you move forward in your journey of faith, remember that the victory is already won. Stay connected to God, keep the portals of heaven open in your life, and continue to share the victory with others. In doing so, you will experience the fullness of life that Jesus promised and see His kingdom come on earth as it is in heaven.

May your life be marked by the continuous flow of God's victory, and may you walk in His power, love, and presence all the days of your life. As you live in victory, may you inspire others to do the same, advancing God's kingdom and bringing His light to a world in need. Remember, you are more than a conqueror through Christ, and His victory is your victory—now and forevermore.

Activation Prayer

Heavenly Father, I thank You for the victory that has been secured for me through the life, death, and resurrection of Jesus Christ. I stand today in the assurance that no weapon formed against me shall prosper and that I am more than a conqueror through Him who loves me.

Lord, I ask for Your strength and wisdom as I face the battles of life. Help me to remain steadfast in faith, to walk in obedience to Your Word, and to rely on the power of Your Spirit. When the enemy comes against me, remind me of the victory I already have in You, and give me the courage to stand firm.

I pray for every believer who is in the midst of a spiritual battle. Surround them with Your peace, fill them with Your power, and assure them of Your presence. May they walk in the reality of Your victory, experiencing Your blessings in every area of their lives.

Father, as I live in victory, use me to be a light to others. May my life testify of Your goodness and draw people closer to You. Help me share the hope and freedom that come from knowing You so that others may also experience the abundant life You have promised.

I give You all the glory, honor, and praise, knowing that the battle is Yours and that the victory is already won. I stand in faith, declaring Your name above every other name, and I trust in Your unchanging promises. In the mighty name of Jesus I pray. Amen.

DID YOU KNOW?

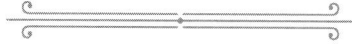

Studies show that gratitude rewires the brain, enhancing well-being and resilience. Living in spiritual victory often includes cultivating gratitude for God's blessings and opening portals to greater joy and fulfillment.

PORTALS IN POP CULTURE:
Dune (2021 film)

Dune provides a metaphorical and visionary take on portals, highlighting spiritual awakening, warfare, and the impact of divine purpose on an individual's life. As this book emphasizes, our call is not just to explore mysteries but to discern them rightly. Remain rooted in Christ, protected by truth, and careful not to wander into realms never meant to be opened.

DARK NIGHT OF THE SOUL

T HE JOURNEY TO living in the victory of heavenly portals is not without its challenges, as we've discovered throughout the previous, power-packed chapters. Among these challenges is what many call the *dark night of the soul*—a profound spiritual concept that describes a period of intense inner struggle and doubt. At times, even believers seem to experience a sense of abandonment by God. This season can feel like spiritual desolation, when the vibrant connection to the divine seems absent. Yet, as difficult as it is, this experience often marks a transformative process—a journey through which one's faith is tested, refined, and ultimately deepened.

The term *dark night of the soul* originates from a sixteenth-century poem by Saint John of the Cross, a Spanish mystic and Carmelite monk. He described this dark night as a journey of purification, stripping away worldly attachments and superficial faith while fostering a deeper intimacy with God. Though painful, it removes distractions and reveals a love that surpasses human understanding.

Scripture offers several parallels. The life of Job stands as a testimony to enduring trials that refine faith. Stripped of family, health, and possessions, Job cried out to God, questioning His presence. Yet through his suffering, Job's understanding of God's sovereignty deepened. Similarly, King David's psalms reveal his raw cries during seasons of anguish. In Psalm 22:1, he lamented, "My God, my God, why have you forsaken me?"—a cry echoed by Jesus on the cross, symbolizing the spiritual agony of separation.

These moments remind us that even in darkness, a heavenly

portal remains open. God's light often shines brightest in the night, transforming the season of trial into a gateway to His glory.

My Own Dark Night of the Soul

Some years ago, my wife and I faced one of the most brutal and challenging seasons of our lives. It was a year of loss and turmoil, filled with crisis that shook us to our core. This season became an actual spiritual reckoning in my life. The place where I had once found comfort and clarity—my prayer room—became my battlefield. I faced overwhelming waves of fear and worry—even pride. The voices of doubt screamed louder than ever, tempting me to let go of my calling, my ministry, and my faith. Everything I had believed and preached about to others was being tested in the fire of this dark night. My reputation was questioned, my character maligned, and my spirit crushed under the weight of accusations, slander, and persecution. In this darkness, there was only one lifeline: crying out to God. Like David, I poured out my heart, unfiltered and raw. His words in the Psalms became my own:

> I am worn out from my groaning. All night long I flood my
> bed with weeping....The Lord has heard my cry for mercy.
> —Psalm 6:6–9

> How long, Lord? Will you forget me forever?...But I
> trust in your unfailing love.
> —Psalm 13:1–5

> My God, my God, why have you forsaken me?...In you
> our ancestors put their trust; they trusted and you deliv-
> ered them.
> —Psalm 22:1–4

Through these verses, I saw a pattern: honesty in despair, the remembrance of God's faithfulness, and, ultimately, a choice to trust Him. They became a road map for me to navigate the darkness and find the portal to His presence.

In the depth of my darkest night, the portal to heaven opened—not in external circumstances but within my spirit. Unlike what I thought I had wanted, God's response to my cries wasn't a miraculous resolution or public vindication. Instead, it was His presence, filling me with a supernatural peace that transcended understanding. His love became my refuge, His voice my anchor, and His presence my only pursuit.

I let go of my long lists of prayer requests and shifted to one singular focus—the "one thing" David spoke of in Psalm 27:4: "One thing I ask from the Lord, this only do I seek: that I may dwell in the house of the Lord all the days of my life." I rediscovered that the portal to victory wasn't found through changing my circumstances. His presence was what I needed the most.

Lessons from the Dark Night

The dark night of the soul stripped away everything I'd once held on to—my plans, my reputation, my ministry—and led me back to the vows I had made to God two decades before. Stripped of everything, I remembered my first love. What felt like my worst season became the setup for my greatest. My darkest night gave birth to my brightest day (in fact, this book was born from that season in my life), and I emerged renewed and restored, ready to get back to His mission for my life. All glory, honor, and praise to Christ Jesus!

I learned some things through that experience that I believe will be a blessing to you.

Be honest with God. Don't hide your pain or doubts. Like David, pour out your heart before Him. God welcomes your raw emotions.

Seek His presence: Answers may not come immediately, but His presence will sustain you. The open portal is found not in solutions but in intimacy with Him.

Remember His faithfulness. Look back at how God has

delivered and sustained you before. Let that history fuel your hope for the future.

Focus on the one thing. Let go of everything else and prioritize His presence. When all else fades, He remains.

Victory Through the Portal

The dark night of the soul is not the end, my friend. I can tell you that it is the doorway to a deeper, more victorious relationship with God. The pain of the night purifies our hearts, drawing us closer to Him and opening the heavenly portal through which His glory is revealed. If you find yourself in such a season, take heart: God has not abandoned you. He is refining your faith, strengthening your spirit, and preparing you for the greater purpose ahead.

When everything else fades, remember this: His presence is enough. His love is enough. Through the open heavenly portal, your darkest night will become the foundation of your brightest victory.

> I would have lost heart, unless I had believed that I would
> see the goodness of the LORD in the land of the living.
> Wait on the LORD; be of good courage, and He shall
> strengthen your heart; wait, I say, on the LORD!
> —PSALM 27:13–14, NKJV

As we reach the end of *Spiritual Portals*, it is my hope that you now stand equipped with a deeper understanding of the spiritual realities that surround us. This book has been a journey into the heart of the unseen, revealing how portals—spiritual gateways—shape our connection to the divine and influence our daily lives.

We began by uncovering the profound truth of heavenly portals, with Jesus Christ as the ultimate gateway to God's presence and blessings. These portals are tangible and accessible to you *today* as you seek His will and move into a deeper relationship with Him. They serve as conduits for His power and presence, which are the only true source of transformation and victory for our lives.

We also explored the sobering reality of demonic portals, the gateways through which darkness seeks to infiltrate our lives and destroy us. By recognizing and discerning these portals, we are empowered to shut them down through repentance, deliverance, and the authority of Jesus Christ.

Through the lens of spiritual warfare, we examined the battle for the soul, emphasizing the critical role of free will in opening and closing portals. We were reminded that what we do in this world is not isolated—it ripples into the spiritual realm, influencing outcomes far beyond what we can see.

Practical strategies filled these pages, from unlocking heavenly portals in your home and church to engaging in prayer and worship as powerful tools for opening the heavens. We were challenged to immerse ourselves in God's Word and strengthen our faith as we actively step into the authority granted to us by Christ. Each chapter offered knowledge, but I have also armed you with the tools you need to navigate the complexities of spiritual portals with wisdom and confidence.

The journey was not without its challenges, as we reflected on the "dark night of the soul" and the trials that test and refine our faith. Yet, even in the darkest moments, the promise of God's presence through an open heavenly portal remains steadfast, guiding us to victory.

The spiritual realities of portals are so important. They are central to the lives of all believers. As you step away from this book and into the battles and blessings of your daily walk, remember this: You have been given the authority to open heavenly portals and close demonic ones. You are not powerless. You are equipped.

Remember to live in the light. Pursue the heavenly portals that bring God's presence and power into your life. Guard against the dark—be vigilant against deception, along with any actions that open doors to the enemy. And walk in authority—claim the victory Christ has already won for you, and share that victory with others.

May this book serve as a reminder of your identity as a child of

God and a warrior in His kingdom. The battle is real, but so is the victory. Every step you take toward opening heavenly portals is a step toward greater intimacy with God and a life of abundance in Christ.

Let me pray for you:

Heavenly Father, I worship You and thank You. I come before You with humility and gratitude. Thank You for never leaving me nor forsaking me, for granting me Your unending love and grace. Thank You for using me—a broken, flawed, and imperfect vessel—to reveal Your perfect Word, nature, and essence. I am grateful for the strength and courage You have given me to endure the most challenging storms, allowing me to see this day and minister to Your precious children.

Father, I pray that every reader of these words is empowered to walk in the victory of heavenly portals. May their eyes be opened to the spiritual realities around them, their hearts steadfast in Your truth, and their lives marked by Your glory. Let no scheme of the enemy prevail against them, for they are Yours. May Your heavenly portals bring life and blessing into their families and communities. May their lives reflect the power of Your kingdom. Lord, we love You and vow to remain faithful in seeking, serving, and worshipping You all the days of our lives. In Jesus' mighty name, amen.

As we conclude, let me leave you with this last encouragement: Heavenly portals are open to those who seek them with faith, diligence, and surrender. Go forward, bold and unshaken, knowing that the heavens are waiting to pour out blessings beyond what you can imagine. The journey is yours—walk in victory.

Until next time… Shalom. Peace, love, and God bless!

A PERSONAL NOTE

FRIEND, THE UNSEEN realm is more real than the ground beneath your feet. Every day, whether we recognize it or not, we are standing in the intersection of two realms—the heavenly and the demonic.

Maybe you've felt lost in life, surrounded by darkness and confusion. Perhaps you have experienced the spiritual heaviness I described while searching for peace in all the wrong places. I want you to know this: **Jesus is the One you've been looking for.** In John 10:9, He declares, **"I am the gate; whoever enters through me will be saved."**

He is the gateway to eternal life—the door through which we must enter to access the presence of God and the blessings of the kingdom. Through His sacrifice on the cross, the Lord Jesus opened the greatest of all heavenly portals, granting us **direct access to the Father**. When you give your life to Him, everything changes: Bondage is broken, purpose is awakened, and heaven opens over your life. Best of all, you receive the most amazing gift of eternal life.

If you're ready to walk through this most important door and enter a relationship with the living God, I invite you to pray this simple prayer from your heart:

> *Lord Jesus, I believe You are the Son of God. I believe You died on the cross for my sins and rose again to give me new life. Today, I turn from darkness and step into the light. Forgive me of my sins. Wash me clean. Fill me with Your presence. I surrender my heart to You and*

*receive You as my Savior and Lord. From this moment on,
I belong to You. Lead me through Your heavenly portals,
and help me walk in Your power and truth every day. In
Jesus' name, amen.*

If you prayed that prayer, all of heaven is rejoicing—and so am I! This is the beginning of a supernatural journey into the presence and power of God. I encourage you to reach out to my publisher at **pray4me@charismamedia.com** so we can bless you with free resources to strengthen your new walk with the Lord Jesus. We'd love to celebrate with you and help you grow in this incredible relationship.

Welcome to the kingdom of God!

WITH LOVE,
SERGIO NAZIR CHAVEZ

ABOUT the AUTHOR

Dynamic powerhouse Sergio Nazir Chavez is an apostolic and prophetic voice to this generation. He is a sought-after speaker, visionary leadership expert, and entrepreneur who has traveled across the United States, Central America, and the Caribbean, engaging the masses with his compelling, dynamic, and transformative messages of hope. He believes that in our current climate, this generation has been appointed to leave behind the greatest legacy and demonstration of God's power that our nation's history has ever seen. His mission is clear: to know Christ and to make Him known! Sergio is married to his best friend and destiny partner, Franchesca Chavez. Together they founded and pastor at Hope Center in Baltimore. They are proud parents of three daughters. Chavez is also the founder and president of Sergio Nazir Chavez Ministries since 2023.

Connect with Sergio Nazir Chavez
www.sergionazirchavez.com
Social media: @sergionazirchavez—Facebook,
Instagram, YouTube, TikTok
admin@sergionazirchavez.com